SUPER HERO MATH AND TECH

BY JENNIFER HACKETT

downtown bookworks

downtown bookworks

Downtown Bookworks Inc.
New York, New York
www.downtownbookworks.com

Designed by Georgia Rucker
Printed in the United States, October 2020
ISBN 978-1-950587-07-0

10 9 8 7 6 5 4 3 2 1

PHOTO CREDITS

62: VikiVector/Shutterstock.com. 77: Africa Studio/Shutterstock.com (drone),
Engineer studio/Shutterstock.com (rescue bot), kung_tom Shutterstock.com (worker bot).
92: Dabarti CGI/Shutterstock.com. 93: Helioscribe/Shutterstock.com (beam bridge), jessica.
kirsh/Shutterstock.com (truss bridge), rodho/Shutterstock.com (arch bridge). 95: Sean Pavone/
Shutterstock.com (Taipei 101), Ilona Ignatova/Shutterstock.com (Burj Khalifa), Hitman H/
Shutterstock.com (Guangzhou CTF Finance Tower). 100: Photo by NASA. 101: Photos by NASA
(top three), ladyfortune/Shutterstock.com (camera lens), ya_blue_ko/Shutterstock.com (glasses),
MoonRock/Shutterstock.com (headset). 103: nobeastsofierce/Shutterstock.com (graphene),
photo by Ecovative Design (mushroom packaging).107: Sashkin/Shutterstock.com (tennis ball),
comodigit/Shutterstock.com (sunscreen), chaphot/Shutterstock.com (waterproof fabric).
108: asharkyu/Shutterstock.com. 109: asharkyu/Shutterstock.com.

ILLUSTRATION CREDITS

Select illustrations by Scott Kolins: Bumblebee (pages 38–39, 41).

Superman created by Jerry Siegel and Joe Shuster. By special arrangement with
the Jerry Siegel family.

CONTENTS

$= \dfrac{4}{5}$

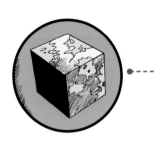

What Is MATH? What Is TECH?

Math, or **MATHEMATICS**, is the study of numbers and shapes. And numbers and shapes are everywhere! You use math when you add up how many pizzas you need for the whole basketball team, buy snacks at the store, or figure out how big a box you need to fit a gift.

Tech, or **TECHNOLOGY**, is the use of math and science to solve problems. Most of the materials, gadgets, and furniture you use every day are types of technology.

Read on to find out how Batman, Wonder Woman, Superman, and your other favorite Super Heroes use math and tech to battle Super-Villains, keep people safe, and make the most of their awesome powers.

Mighty MATHEMATICS

Robin patrols the streets of Gotham City so he can report back to Batman. As he hops from roof to roof, he counts **5** bank robbers and **2** groups of **4** police officers. He knows that **8** police officers is **3** more than **5** bank robbers, so he moves along. The police officers can handle them!

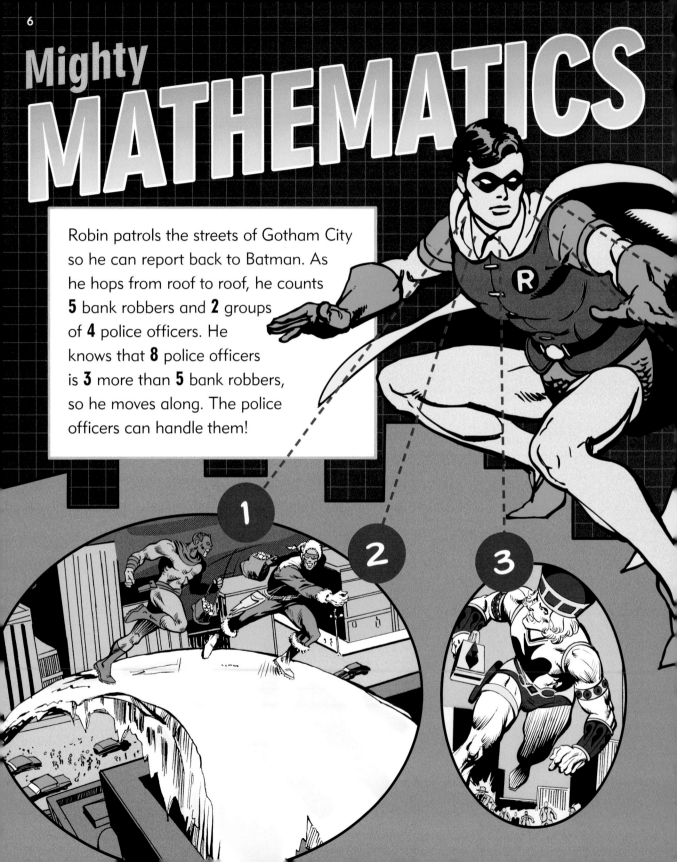

Robin is using math to keep his city safe. Any time Robin counts, adds, or multiplies, he's using math. Addition and multiplication are **OPERATIONS**. Operations are a way to combine different numbers. They can be combined to find the total number of things in any given situation.

Robin can count by **1**s, **2**s, or any number he likes. He can take away from what he's counted with subtraction, or double it by adding the same amount to itself. Understanding when to use what operation is an important skill for Robin when he's on patrol!

Robin's TIPS and TRICKS

While keeping the streets of Gotham City safe, Robin has to think fast. That's why he's mastered many tricks to make things easier and quicker. As he leaps above a group of thieves, he counts them in groups of **2** to know how many he's dealing with.

When sorting Batarangs to see which ones needs to be repaired, he groups them in piles of **5** so he knows at a glance how many he has. And he has the sum of all digits less than **10** memorized from constant practice!

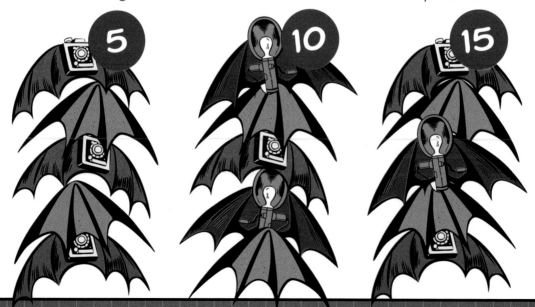

10, 20, 30, 40, 50, 60, 70 . . .

B-BATGIRL....?!

Other Super Heroes use groups of numbers too. When Batgirl works out, she counts her kicks by **10**s.

The Green Lanterns like to count by **20**s while they wait for their rings to be fully charged.

20, 40, 60, 80 . . .

Try It! When you have a lot of things to count, counting by ones takes a long time! Counting by set numbers, like Robin does, is a great way to quickly count large groups of items or people. Try it out yourself! What's the largest number you can count to in 30 seconds? Set a timer and see!

When counting by **1**s:

When counting by **2**s:

When counting by **5**s:

When counting by **10**s:

When counting by **20**s:

When counting by **100**s:

Amazing ADDITION

Aquaman uses his power to communicate with marine life. No matter where he is in the ocean, he's only one call away from sea creatures. He calls **8** fish to join him. He then calls **12** more. How many fish does he have altogether?

One way Aquaman can find the number of fish in his group is by counting each fish. Hope he doesn't lose track of who he's already counted!

He can also use a number line! It's a bit easier than keeping track of all those swimming fish. When adding using a number line, you move from left to right. First count out **8** spaces on the line. Then count **12** more. Where on the line do you end up?

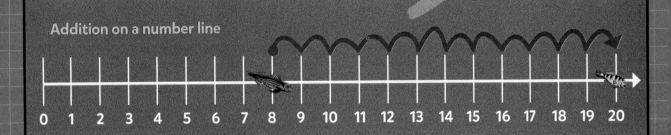

Addition on a number line

0 1 2 3 4 5 6 7 8 9 10 11 12 13 14 15 16 17 18 19 20

Or Aquaman can determine how many fish he has in his group now by using **ADDITION**. Addition is when you combine two or more numbers to find their total, or **SUM**. Here is how Aquaman can set up an addition problem:

Setting up an addition problem like this helps Aquaman organize the numbers so they are easier to work with. He starts with the numbers on the right. He knows that **2 + 8 = 10**. And he knows that **10 + 10** equals **20**!

No matter which way he adds up the numbers, the answer is the same.

$$\begin{array}{r} 12 \\ + 8 \\ \hline \end{array}$$

Stunning SUBTRACTION

Sometimes it's hard to navigate the ocean with a big crowd of fish! So Aquaman sends **7** of his finned friends away. He can find how many fish are left in his group using **SUBTRACTION**.

Subtraction is when you take one number away from another to find your new total, which is called the **DIFFERENCE**. Subtraction is the opposite of addition.

To find his new, smaller total, Aquaman can cross off the fish he's taking away. Using the counting method, he can count out **7** fish to leave. Then he can count the remaining fish.

He can also turn back to his trusty tool, the number line!
When subtracting using a number line, move from right to left.

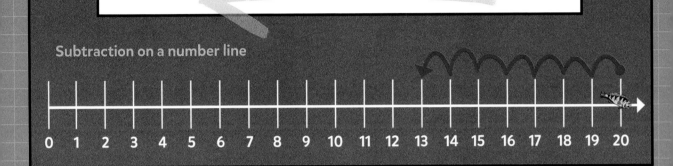

Subtraction on a number line

0 1 2 3 4 5 6 7 8 9 10 11 12 13 14 15 16 17 18 19 20

Aquaman can also set up a subtraction problem.

He can break his subtraction problem into groups of **10**.

- Aquaman knows **20** is **2** groups of **10**.
- He also knows **10 – 7** is **3**.
- That leaves one group of **10** and one group of **3**, which means he has **13** fish left with him!

WHICH WAY OF DOING SUBTRACTION DO YOU LIKE THE MOST?

20
– 7

POSITIVE and NEGATIVE

Mera can swim through the ocean in any direction. She can swim up, toward the surface, or she can swim down, toward the ocean floor.

Mera can think about the direction she swims as being **POSITIVE** or **NEGATIVE**. A positive number is greater than zero. A negative number is less than zero. Negative numbers have minus signs in front of them, like **−5**, **−10**, **−20**. Think of where Mera starts in the ocean as zero on a vertical number line.

If Mera starts at 0 and swims a positive 20 feet, where will she be?

If Mera starts at 0 and swims a NEGATIVE 13 feet, where will she be?

Mera won't always start out at 0. If Mera swims up 10 feet, she swims to POSITIVE 10. If she swims down 15 feet from there, she swims to NEGATIVE 5.

Try It!

Answers on page 112.

1. If Mera starts at **0** and swims a **POSITIVE 6** feet, and then a **NEGATIVE 9** feet where will she be?

2. If Mera starts at **NEGATIVE 5** and swims a **POSITIVE 12** feet, where will she be?

3. If Mera starts at **POSITIVE 14** and swims a **NEGATIVE 11** feet, where will she be?

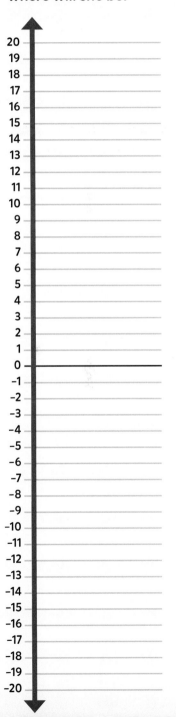

MULTIPLICATION Mayhem

Super Heroes know there's strength in numbers. That's why Martian Manhunter's ability to multiply himself is so powerful. By making copies of himself, Martian Manhunter can become a one-man army. Fighting one Super Hero is tough, but try taking on **20** at once!

When Martian Manhunter **MULTIPLIES**, he's doing repeated addition. If he multiplies himself **10** times, he ends up with **10** copies of himself, or **1** times **10**.

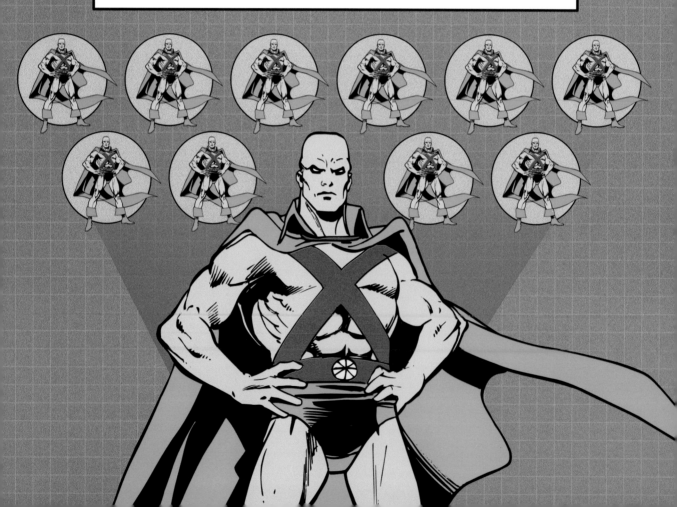

You can use an **ARRAY** to show how many copies of Martian Manhunter there are. An array is an arrangement of items in columns and rows that make it easy to model multiplication problems. For example, you can show **10** Super Heroes by arranging them in **1** row and **10** columns. Or you can show them in **2** rows and **5** columns.

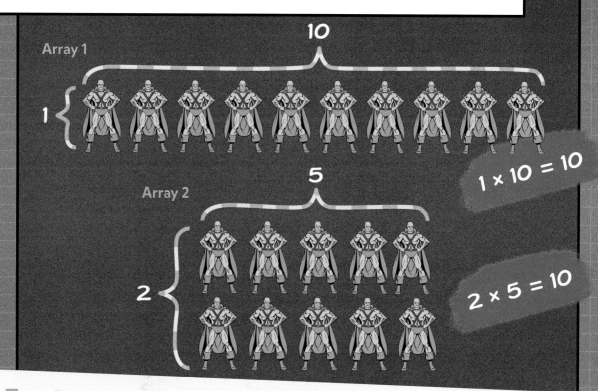

Array 1

10

1

$1 \times 10 = 10$

Array 2

5

2

$2 \times 5 = 10$

Try It! Martian Manhunter multiplies himself to match the number of enemies he's fighting. Finish the multiplication sentence to help him know how many multiples he needs!

Answers on page 112.

1.
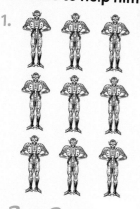

$3 \times 3 =$

2.

$2 \times 4 =$

3.

$4 \times 2 =$

Dynamic DIVISION

Now that Martian Manhunter has multiplied himself, he can break up into groups to tackle different challenges.

If he splits into equal groups, Martian Manhunter is using **DIVISION**. Division is the opposite of multiplication. Just like multiplication is repeated addition, division is repeated subtraction.

One way he can determine how many copies should be in each group is by taking one copy from the main group and adding it to each new group over and over until he runs out. If he wants **3** even groups, he would take away **1** copy and add it to the first group, then take away another copy to add to the second group, and **1** more to add to the third group. Martian Manhunter can do this until there are no more copies left to split up.

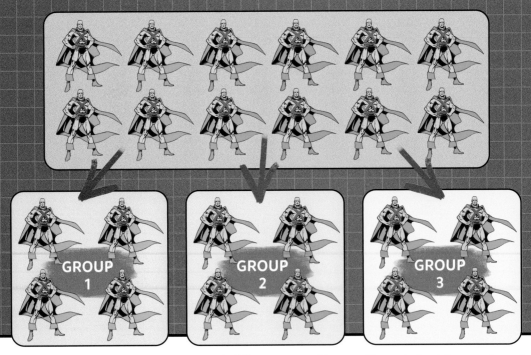

If Martian Manhunter starts with **12** copies of himself and decides to break into **3** groups, each group will have **4** copies.

Division can also be shown using an array. For example, **12** Super Heroes can be shown in **3** groups of **4**. They can also be shown in **2** groups of **6**.

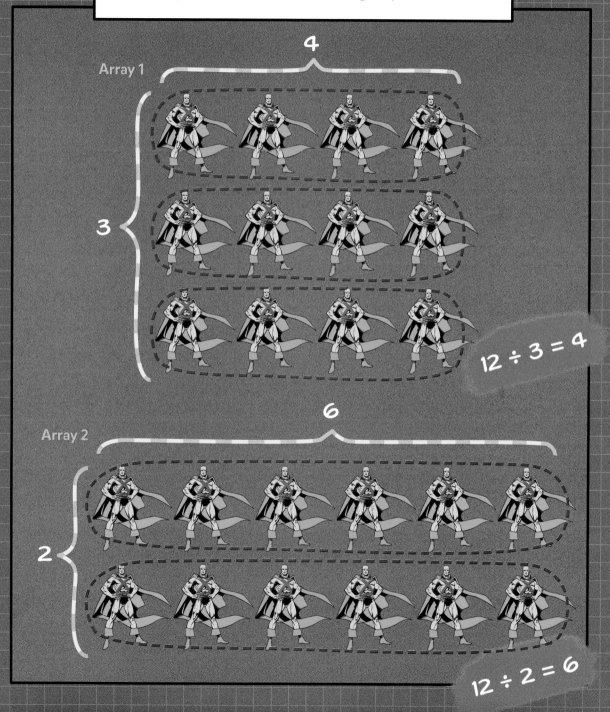

Try It!

Martian Manhunter divides his copies to address different numbers of villains who are up to no good throughout the city.

Answers on page 112.

----

1. Martian Manhunter has 9 copies. He wants to send equal numbers to battle 3 different villains. How many copies does he send after each troublemaker?

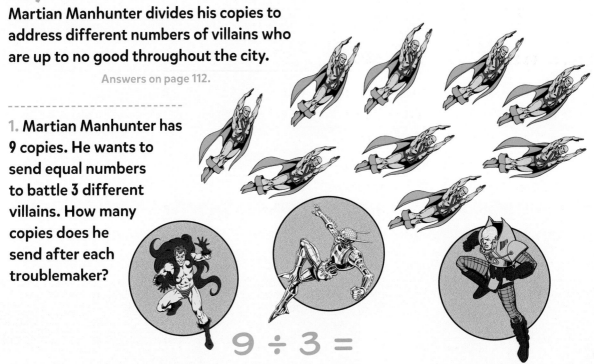

$$9 \div 3 =$$

----

2. Uh-oh! Now there are 5 Super-Villains! Martian Manhunter has 15 copies. To send an equal number of copies after each criminal, he must do some math. How many Martian Manhunters will battle each baddie?

$$15 \div 5 =$$

ORDER Matters

When you add and multiply, order doesn't matter. Martian Manhunter knows that **3 + 1** is the same as **1 + 3** and that **2 × 4** is the same as **4 × 2**.

But the same is not true of subtraction and division! Martian Manhunter never mixes up **4 ÷ 2**, which equals **2**, with **2 ÷ 4**, which equals $\frac{1}{2}$. Be careful, and don't mix up your numbers!

PARTS OF AN EQUATION

The parts of an equation have their own names.

FACTORS: Numbers multiplied together to get a new number

PRODUCT: The result of multiplication

$$2 \times 5 = 10$$

DIVIDEND: The number being divided

DIVISOR: The number you are dividing by

QUOTIENT: The result of division

$$8 \div 4 = 2$$

Translating WORD PROBLEMS

When he shoots an arrow, Green Arrow has to think through many things. He has to determine how far his arrow will fly. He needs to decide how far back to draw his bow. He needs to quickly figure out what information is important to help him hit his target.

Green Arrow approaches word problems the same way. He reads the problem to understand what's being asked. He underlines key words and circles important numbers. If there's extra information that distracts him, he crosses it out.

To know what a question is asking, Green Arrow looks for keywords or phrases. Words like "increased by" or "combined" mean that **ADDITION** takes place. Words like "less than" or "difference" mean **SUBTRACTION**. "Times" or "groups of" means **MULTIPLICATION**, and "split" or "divided equally" can mean **DIVISION**. Looking for these keywords helps him know what operation to perform. Here are some examples. Can you come up with an equation for each word problem?

Try It!

1. Green Arrow never misses his mark because he's always practicing! He set up ⑩ targets for practice. He has ⑭ arrows in his quiver. What is the **DIFFERENCE** between the number of targets he set up and the number of arrows he has?

2. To hit multiple foes at once, Green Arrow shoots ⑤ arrows **AT A TIME**. He shoots ③ **GROUPS** of arrows. How many arrows does he shoot?

3. Sometimes groups of Super Heroes **SPLIT UP** to cover more ground. Once Green Arrow was working as part of a team of ⑥. The group decided to **SPLIT UP** into ③ **EQUAL GROUPS**. How many Super Heroes are in each group?

Answers on page 112.

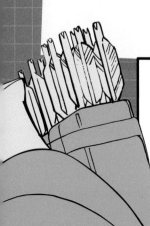

To make sure he hits his target, Green Lantern always checks his work. That means he thinks about his answer to make sure it makes sense. For example, if he's trying to split his arrows evenly between **3** quivers, he knows his answer is reasonable if each quiver ends up with the same number of arrows.

WORD PROBLEM POWER

Try It! Practice your word-problem powers with these super questions!

Answers on page 112.

1. Someone has shrunk Wonder Woman! Normally, Wonder Woman is **68** inches tall. After being shrunken down, she's **62** inches less than her normal height. How tall, in inches, is Wonder Woman after she is downsized?

2. Batman is always prepared with a costume. No matter what color costume he wears, it has a cowl, a cape, a belt, a suit, and a pair of boots. That's **5** parts for each costume! If he has a different-colored costume for each day of the week, how many costume parts does he have in total?

3. Oh no! The Justice League and the Justice Society have been captured! And the Green Lanterns from both teams have to save everyone! There are 8 Super Heroes trapped in 4 space prisons. There's an equal number of Super Heroes in each prison. How many Super Heroes are in each prison?

4. It would take 100 people to lift the key to Superman's Fortress of Solitude. Superman's key weighs 4,000 pounds. Each person lifting it supports the same amount of weight. How much weight is each person holding up?

Now you give it a shot! Look at the picture and write a word problem about the Justice League.

PRIME Numbers

The Justice League is made up of **7** Super Heroes. Most problems are handled by **5** of the **7**. And **3** of the **7** are some of the most famous Super Heroes in the world!

Each of these numbers is a special type of number called a **PRIME NUMBER**. A prime number can't be divided by any whole number other than itself and **1**. It doesn't have any other factors, or numbers that can be multiplied together that result in it.

There is only one number array that works with the number **5**:

There is only one number array that works with the number **7**:

Here are all the other prime numbers up to 100:

2 3 5 7 11 13 17 19 23 29 31 37 41 43
47 53 59 61 67 71 73 79 83 89 97

You will notice that the number **2** is the only **EVEN NUMBER** in the bunch. All other prime numbers are **ODD NUMBERS**. Why is that? It's because all other even numbers have a factor of **2**.

EVENS AND ODDS

EVEN numbers can be evenly divided by 2. **ODD** numbers cannot be divided by 2. A team of 4 can neatly split into 2 groups, so it's **EVEN**. But a team of 7 can't, so it's **ODD**!

Try It! The Flash needs to get to the rest of his team. Guide him to Batman by following the path marked by EVEN numbers! (He can only move up and down, left and right, not diagonal!)   Answers on page 112.

2	7	15	12	4	9	40	6	22	12	89	7	90	14	74
44	2	78	12	5	14	30	37	12	7	8	10	68	39	96
9	45	17	4	65	12	11	27	88	50	12	31	12	41	100
12	13	81	8	77	66	21	98	13	71	55	24	8	91	11
5	7	11	12	20	54	33	2	6	12	79	99	47	75	85

Aquaman needs to get back to Storm, his trusty seahorse. Guide him to Storm by following the path of ODD numbers! (Again, he can only move up, down, right or left.)

12	7	15	12	4	10	87	6	22	12	13	93	45	9	50
44	2	78	64	5	77	79	37	12	7	17	16	68	39	6
1	45	17	4	65	12	2	27	88	55	12	31	12	41	22
12	10	81	90	77	66	21	35	13	71	40	24	8	91	9
5	7	11	13	21	54	83	2	6	64	79	33	20	56	99

Order of OPERATIONS

During a big battle, Super Heroes have to be smart as well as strong! It's important that they do their jobs in the right order. For example, Robin needs to get into the Batmobile *before* Batman drives away. Batman can only scale the building *after* he secures the bat rope.

Just like Batman has to do things in the right sequence, he has to solve a problem with multiple operations in the right sequence too. This is called the **ORDER OF OPERATIONS**. It's a fancy name for solving problems in the right order.

THE ORDER IS:

PARENTHESIS, OR GROUPS: First, tackle any operations you find inside parentheses.

$$(8+6) \times (4-2) \div 7$$

EXPONENTS: Exponents looks like this 2^2 and 4^3. You don't need to worry about exponents just yet.

MULTIPLICATION AND DIVISION, FROM LEFT TO RIGHT: Moving from left to right, do all of the multiplication and division problems in the order you reach them.

ADDITION AND SUBTRACTION, FROM LEFT TO RIGHT: Moving from left to right, do all of the addition and subtraction problems in the order you reach them.

Batman uses the **ORDER** to tackle a tricky foe — this math problem!

$$(8+6) \times (4-2) \div 7$$

First, he must solve what's in the parentheses, or groups. That means he adds **8** and **6** to get **14**. Then he subtracts **2** from **4** to get **2**. The equation is now:

$$14 \times 2 \div 7$$

Batman then multiples **14** by **2**, because the multiplication sign comes before the division sign when going left to right. **14 × 2** is **28**, so that makes the equation:

$$28 \div 7$$

Finally, he divides **28** by **7** to get the final answer of **4**.

$$28 \div 7 = 4$$

If Batman hadn't followed the order of operations, he would have been very confused—and may have wound up with the wrong answer!

THANKS, ORDER OF OPERATIONS!

Fearless FRACTIONS

Many Super Heroes work in teams. Different members of the team have different powers. The Birds of Prey is a team of Super Heroes made up of Huntress, Black Canary, and Oracle. They work together to form a powerful group, but also work on their own sometimes. Each Super Hero represents a **FRACTION** of the whole team.

A fraction is a part of a whole. That means it can represent something less than **1**, where the number **1** represents the whole group. Each member of the Birds of Prey is an equal part of the team, so each member is $\frac{1}{3}$ of the whole team. Black Canary is $\frac{1}{3}$ of the Birds of Prey.

One-third can be written as:

And it can be modeled as:

$$\frac{1}{3}$$

When you're working with groups of heroes, it's important to know how to use fractions to make the most of your team!

BATMAN IS $\frac{1}{3}$ OF HIS TEAM.

PARTS of a Whole

The Justice League is made up of many different Super Heroes. Some can fly, while others have super-strength. But each Super Hero is an equal part of the team.

The total number of Super Heroes in the Justice League makes up a whole. That means that **7** out of **7** Super Heroes, or $\frac{7}{7}$, represents the whole team.

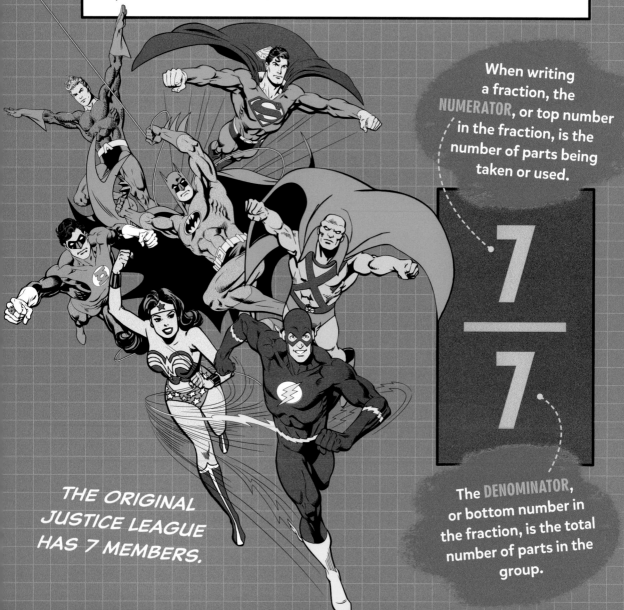

When writing a fraction, the **NUMERATOR**, or top number in the fraction, is the number of parts being taken or used.

$$\frac{7}{7}$$

THE ORIGINAL JUSTICE LEAGUE HAS 7 MEMBERS.

The **DENOMINATOR**, or bottom number in the fraction, is the total number of parts in the group.

You can use **FRACTIONS** to compare parts of the Justice League to the whole, or the total number of Super Heroes in the League. In the Justice League, Superman and Martian Manhunter, **2** out of the **7** members, are aliens. You can write that as:

$$\frac{2}{7}$$ MEMBERS OF THE JUSTICE LEAGUE ARE ALIENS.

Martian Manhunter, Green Lantern, Wonder Woman, and Superman can fly. You can write that as:

$$\frac{4}{7}$$ MEMBERS OF THE JUSTICE LEAGUE CAN FLY.

COMPARING Fractions

Now that you know how to represent parts of a whole as a fraction, it is easy to compare fractions to one another. Are there more aliens in the Justice League than there are Super Heroes who can fly? Since $\frac{4}{7}$ refers to the number of members of the Justice League who can fly and $\frac{2}{7}$ refers to the number of members of the Justice League that are aliens, the answer is clear. $\frac{4}{7}$ is greater than $\frac{2}{7}$. There are more members who can fly!

$$\frac{4}{7} \quad IS \quad GREATER \quad THAN \quad \frac{2}{7}$$

Another way to show that one number is GREATER THAN another is to use this symbol >.

$$\frac{4}{7} > \frac{2}{7}$$

The symbol for LESS THAN is <.

$$\frac{2}{7} < \frac{4}{7}$$

If two whole numbers or fractions are THE SAME, use =.

$$\frac{5}{7} = \frac{5}{7}$$

Try It! On a separate sheet of paper, answer the following questions in fraction form:

- How many members of the Justice League have super-strength?
- How many have red boots?
- How many have blue boots?
- How many wear capes?
- How many wear masks?
- Compare fractions about the Justice League using the words "greater than," "less than," and "equal to."

It is pretty easy to compare fractions when they have the **SAME DENOMINATOR**. But how do you compare compare groups when the total number of members (the denominators) are different?

The Justice League has **7** regular members, and the Teen Titans have **5**. Both teams are made up of a mix of aliens and people from Earth: **5** members of the Justice League are from Earth, and **4** members of the Teen Titans are from Earth. Which team has a greater fraction of members from Earth?

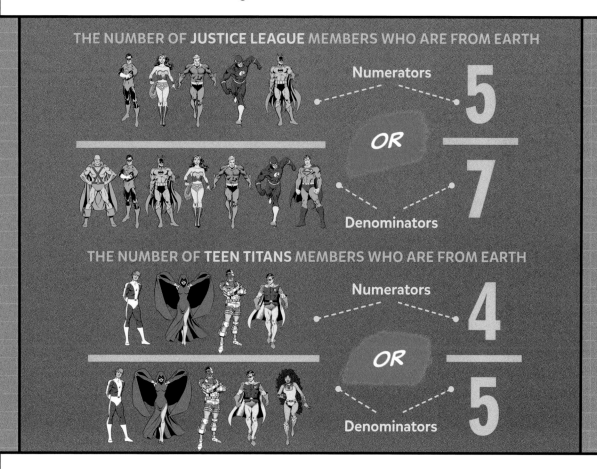

THE NUMBER OF **JUSTICE LEAGUE** MEMBERS WHO ARE FROM EARTH

Numerators

OR

$\dfrac{5}{7}$

Denominators

THE NUMBER OF **TEEN TITANS** MEMBERS WHO ARE FROM EARTH

Numerators

OR

$\dfrac{4}{5}$

Denominators

To compare fractions with different denominators, you can change fractions so they have the same denominator! The denominator for the Justice League is **7**. The denominator for Teen Titans is **5**. You just need to find the **LEAST COMMON MULTIPLE** of **7** and **5**. **35** is the smallest number that is divisible by both **7** and **5**. When you put it on the bottom of each of the fractions, it is the **LEAST COMMON DENOMINATOR**.

Here's how you change the fraction that represents the number of Justice League members who are from Earth ($\frac{5}{7}$) into a fraction with a denominator of **35**.

THE NUMBER OF JUSTICE LEAGUE MEMBERS WHO ARE FROM EARTH

OR $\frac{5}{7}$

$$\frac{5}{7} \times \frac{\square}{\square} = \frac{\square}{35}$$

To change $\frac{5}{7}$ into a fraction with a denominator of 35, you need to multiply the bottom number by 5.

$$\frac{5}{7} \times \frac{\square}{5} = \frac{\square}{35}$$

But it's important to remember that whatever you do to the denominator, you must do to the numerator too! If you multiply the bottom number by 5, you must also multiply the top number by 5. That way the fraction stays the same.

$$\frac{5}{7} \times \frac{5}{5} = \frac{\square}{35}$$

And the new fraction is:

$$\frac{5}{7} \times \frac{5}{5} = \frac{25}{35}$$

Now, it's time to transform the Teen Titans fraction. What number do you need to use to turn the Teen Titans into a fraction with a denominator of **35**?

THE NUMBER OF **TEEN TITANS** MEMBERS WHO ARE FROM EARTH

OR $\dfrac{4}{5}$

$$\dfrac{4}{5} \times \dfrac{\square}{\square} = \dfrac{\square}{35}$$

To turn $\frac{4}{5}$ into a fraction with a denominator of 35, you need to multiply the bottom number by 7.

$$\dfrac{4}{5} \times \dfrac{\square}{7} = \dfrac{\square}{35}$$

You multiplied the denominator by 7. So you need to multiply the numerator by 7 too.

$$\dfrac{4}{5} \times \dfrac{7}{7} = \dfrac{\square}{35}$$

And the new fraction is:

$$\dfrac{4}{5} \times \dfrac{7}{7} = \dfrac{28}{35}$$

Now that the two fractions have the same denominator, they are easy to compare. Since $\frac{28}{35}$ is greater than $\frac{25}{35}$, the Teen Titans have a greater fraction of humans on the team than the Justice League.

WHOLE NUMBERS and FRACTIONS

Whether the problem is big or small, Bumblebee can always face it head on. That's because she can change her size! Bumblebee can **SCALE** herself down to a fraction of her normal size. That means she can shrink to only a tiny part of her full size and slip by unnoticed or sneak through tiny cracks. At her normal height, Bumblebee is about **66** inches tall. Her normal height is a **WHOLE NUMBER**. It is not a fraction or a decimal. It represents the total number of inches that make up her height. Each inch is counted.

DON'T FORGET YOUR UNITS!

If you were only told Bumbleebee was 66 tall, would that tell you anything? No! A number without UNITS does not describe a measurement. A unit is a quantity, like inches or pounds, used as a measurement. It tells you how many of a thing you have. In this case, Bumblebee is 66 INCHES tall.

If Bumblebee shrinks down to only $\frac{1}{11}$ of her normal height, what is Bumblebee's new height? You can multiply whole numbers by a fraction to find the answer!

First, you need to turn your whole number into a fraction. You can do this by putting your whole number over the number **1**. The number **66** becomes the numerator, and **1** is the denominator. $\frac{66}{1}$ is the same as **66**.

$$\frac{66}{1}$$

Next, set up your equation.

$$\frac{66}{1} \times \frac{1}{11} = \frac{\boxed{}}{\boxed{}} \text{ INCHES}$$

Then, multiply the numerators together and the denominators together.

$$\frac{66}{1} \times \frac{1}{11} = \frac{66}{11} \text{ INCHES}$$

Congratulations. You've found the answer! When Bumblebee shrinks to $\frac{1}{11}$ of her normal size, she is $\frac{66}{11}$ inches tall. (Don't forget the unit of measure!) But wait! You're not done yet. You can still simplify the fraction.

When a fraction's numerator and denominator have a common factor, you can simplify it. Why simplify? It makes your fraction answers easier to understand. Right now, you know Bumblebee is $\frac{66}{11}$ inches tall. But that is hard to picture. How many inches is that, really? If you simplify this fraction, you can find out.

Both **66** and **11** are divisible by **11**. If you divide both the numerator and the denominator by 11, you will have a simplified fraction!

The value of $\frac{11}{11}$ is 1. So it is like dividing $\frac{66}{11}$ by the number 1. When you simplify a fraction, the numbers get simpler, but the value stays the same.

$$\frac{66}{11} \div \frac{11}{11} = \frac{6}{1} \text{ INCHES}$$

But you're not done yet. This fraction can be made even simpler! Remember that when you have a denominator of one, that means you actually have a whole number, because the fraction says you have **6** parts of a whole of **1**. That means you really have a whole number, **6**!

So Bumblebee is only 6 inches tall. She would be easy to miss at such a small height!

$$\frac{6}{1} = 6 \text{ INCHES}$$

VALUE

The fraction $\frac{3}{6}$ can be simplified since both 3 and 6 have a factor of 3. When you simplify the fraction, you divide both the numerator and the denominator by 3, like this: $\frac{3}{6} \div \frac{3}{3} = \frac{1}{2}$ And when you simplify a fraction, the value of the fraction does not change. Here's a way to show that in pictures. See how $\frac{3}{6}$ is the same as $\frac{1}{2}$?

3 out of 6 boxes are red.   1 out of 2 boxes is red.

Let's practice some more. Bumblebee can fly with her specially designed robotic wings. Her wingspan is about $\frac{2}{3}$ of her total height. How long are her wings?

Since you know Bumblebee is **66** inches tall, you can multiply **66** inches by $\frac{2}{3}$ to find out.

$$\frac{66}{1} \times \frac{2}{3} = \frac{132}{3}$$

Don't forget to simplify! Both **66** and **3** are divisible by **3**.

$$\frac{132}{3} \div \frac{3}{3} = \frac{44}{1} \text{ INCHES}$$

Bumblebee's regular wingspan is **44** inches. When she shrinks down, her wingspan is still $\frac{2}{3}$ of her total height. That total height is just smaller!

Try it! Let's simplify these fractions. First, determine the common factor for each fraction. Then use your skills to simplify.

Answers on page 112.

1. $\frac{3}{6} \div \underline{} = \underline{}$ INCHES

2. $\frac{10}{2} \div \underline{} = \underline{}$ INCHES

3. $\frac{15}{30} \div \underline{} = \underline{}$ INCHES

4. $\frac{4}{16} \div \underline{} = \underline{}$ INCHES

MEASURING Up

The Atom knows a lot about size. That's because he can change his in the blink of an eye! He can go from a normal-sized man to one as tiny as an atom. Depending on how big or small he is, he uses different units of measurement to understand the world around him.

Because the Atom mainly changes his height, he spends a lot of time with units of measurement that deal with length or height. The Atom is a scientist, so he uses the **METRIC SYSTEM** of measurement.

Atom invented a shrinking machine. He tested it on a chair that was 92 centimeters tall.

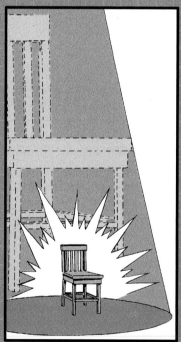

He zapped the chair. His shrinking machine worked!

Now the chair is only 15 centimeters tall!

The metric system is based on powers of **10**. When he's really, really tiny, the Atom uses **MILLIMETERS** to measure his height. If he's a bit bigger—say the size of your hand—he uses **CENTIMETERS**. At his normal adult height, he might use **METERS**, and if he were to get really, really big, he'd use **KILOMETERS**. The metric system is based on multiples of **10**.

This is how big a millimeter is.

This is how big a centimeter is.

CENTIMETER RULER

METRIC SYSTEM CONVERSION

10 MILLIMETERS = 1 CENTIMETER

100 CENTIMETERS = 1 METER

1,000 METERS = 1 KILOMETER

Try It!

Which units would Atom want to use to measure a sofa? A movie poster? A soccer field? A strawberry?

Name some things you would measure in millimeters.

Name some things you would measure in centimeters.

Name some things you would measure in meters.

How about kilometers?

Atom's friends, who aren't scientists, might use a different set of units. People in the United States use the **CUSTOMARY SYSTEM**, which includes **INCHES**, **FEET**, **YARDS**, and **MILES**.

This is how big an inch is.

Just like Beast Boy can transform into all sorts of wild animals, lengths like inches and feet can be transformed, or converted, into other units of measurement.

CUSTOMARY SYSTEM CONVERSION

1 FOOT (FT) = 12 INCHES (IN.)

1 YARD (YD) = 36 INCHES (IN.)

1 YARD (YD) = 3 FEET (FT)

1 MILE (MI) = 5,280 FEET (FT)

1 MILE (MI) = 1,760 YARDS (YD)

12 inches = 1 foot

Try It!

Which units would Atom use to measure the following things?

HIS NORMAL HEIGHT:

Metric: **Customary:**

HIS HEIGHT WHEN SHRUNK TO THE SIZE OF AN INSECT:

Metric: **Customary:**

THE DISTANCE BETWEEN THE EARTH AND THE SUN:

Metric: **Customary:**

ESTIMATING Measurements

Super Heroes and Super-Villains come in all sizes. Some are incredibly tall, and others are itty-bitty! When Super Heroes land on the scene, they need to size up their opponents. One way a hero can get a feel for an enemy is by estimating their size, starting with their height.

Robin is often the shortest hero in the room. He is **5 FEET, 2 INCHES** tall, or **5'2"**. His height is much less than Batman or Superman's. Starfire, on the other hand, tends to tower over others. She is **6 FEET, 4 INCHES** tall, or **6'4"**. She is taller than Aquaman or The Flash!

When you look at these heroes, you can take all the information you have to **ESTIMATE** their height. That's a rough guess about how tall each hero (or pet) is. With the right tools, you can find out exactly how tall each one is!

Try It! Using the information you have, how tall do you think each Super Hero or Super-Villain is? (Remember—height is how tall a person is. You don't have to include hats, hair, or bat ears in a Super Hero's or Super-Villain's height!)

Superman

Krypto

Batman

Hawkgirl

Green Lantern

Wonder Woman

Martian Manhunter

Batgirl

Penguin

Look on page 112 to find out how tall they are. How close were your estimates?

KEY
On this page, 1 foot is equal to this line:

HOT and COLD

Superman knows how to turn up the heat. With his powerful heat vision, he can increase the **TEMPERATURE** of whatever he looks at. If he wants to make things colder, he can use his icy freeze breath to lower the temperature.

HMM...THIS IS THE ONLY WAY TO SLICE THE SUPER-THREAD -- BY HAVING CLARK USE HIS HEAT VISION AT FULL POWER TO BURN IT APART!

SNAP!

Temperature is a measure of how hot or how cold something is. When you check to see what the weather is like, you're looking to see what the day's temperature is. It's usually measured in degrees **FAHRENHEIT** (°F) or degrees **CELSIUS** (°C). In the United States, people use the Fahrenheit scale. Outside the United States, most people use the Celsius scale. One way to find temperature is to read a **THERMOMETER**, which is a device that measures temperature.

THERMOMETERS

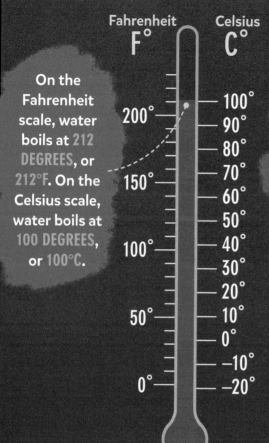

On the Fahrenheit scale, water boils at 212 DEGREES, or 212°F. On the Celsius scale, water boils at 100 DEGREES, or 100°C.

On the Fahrenheit scale, water freezes at 32 DEGREES, or 32°F. On the Celsius scale, water freezes at 0 DEGREES, or 0°C.

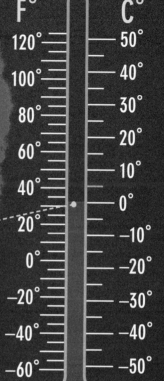

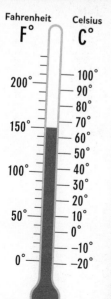

Try It! Show off your thermometer reading skills. The air near the monsters' fire breath is scorching! How hot?

Answers on page 112.

Fahrenheit: **Celsius:**

Grand GEOMETRY

In his Batcave, Batman keeps track of many things. He makes sure there is plenty of air in the tires of the Batmobile so they stay round. He practices throwing his Batarang at different angles so he always knows how to hit his target. He checks where his friends are on a map. All of these things involve **GEOMETRY**, a type of math that studies **POINTS, LINES, SHAPES,** and **ANGLES**!

Your day-to-day life is full of geometry too. The cup you drink from, the lines of your school's hallways, the size and shape of your backpack—it all has to do with geometry. Just like Batman, you can use geometry to understand the world around you.

LINES

In geometry, a LINE is always straight. Lines don't bend. And there are different types of lines.

PARALLEL LINES

When flying side by side, Wonder Woman and Hawkgirl create PARALLEL LINES. Parallel lines will never intersect, or cross over each other. When they fly in parallel lines, Wonder Woman and Hawkgirl know they'll never crash!

When Wonder Woman and Hawkgirl are not flying in parallel lines, they know they will INTERSECT, or cross over one another. When two lines intersect, they make angles.

INTERSECTING LINES

Exploring ANGLES

If Wonder Woman's and Hawkgirl's paths intersect at a **90** degree angle, they make a set of PERPENDICULAR LINES. Their flight path looks like a perfect plus sign.

PERPENDICULAR LINES

Their perpendicular paths create a RIGHT ANGLE, which is an angle that measures **90 DEGREES**, or 90°.

PARTS OF AN ANGLE

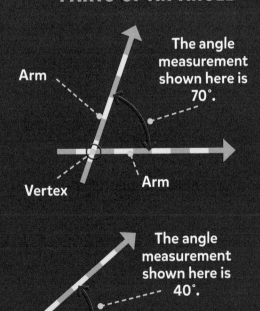

Arm

The angle measurement shown here is 70°.

Vertex

Arm

The angle measurement shown here is 40°.

The two lines that make up an **ANGLE** are called **ARMS**.

The place where the two lines meet is called the **VERTEX**.

The space between the two arms of an angle is the **ANGLE MEASUREMENT**, which is measured in **DEGREES**.

When two lines intersect, it creates all kinds of angles. An angle with a measurement of less than **90** degrees is an **ACUTE** angle.

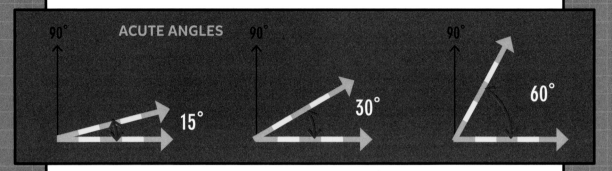

ACUTE ANGLES

90°   15°

90°   30°

90°   60°

An angle with a measurement greater than **90** degrees is called an **OBTUSE** angle.

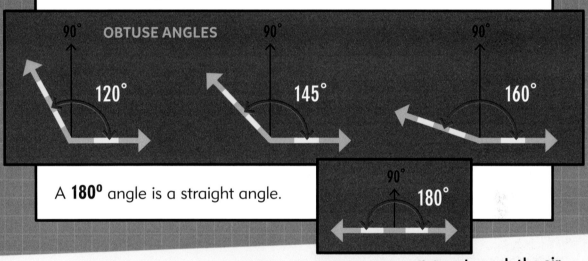

OBTUSE ANGLES

90°   120°

90°   145°

90°   160°

A **180°** angle is a straight angle.

90°   180°

Try It! Wonder Woman and Hawkgirl spent the morning flying through the air. Their paths intersected a bunch of times. Follow the paths and look at the angles. Point to the acute angles. Then find the obtuse angles. Can you find a right angle too?

Answers on page 112.

SHAPES and SIZES

With his stretchy body, Plastic Man can make just about any shape. He can roll down a hill as a giant circle, bend himself into a pointy triangle, or become a big rectangle. It's a good thing Plastic Man knows his **POLYGONS**!

Polygons are figures made up of straight lines, with no gaps. They're often named for the number of sides they have. For example, squares and rectangles are also called quadrilaterals, because they have four sides, and "quad" means four. And the size of a polygon does not change what shape it is. No matter how tiny or how huge a square is, it still has four equal sides.

Polygons can be **REGULAR** or **IRREGULAR**. Polygons are regular when all their side measurements are equal and all their angle measurements are equal. Irregular shapes have different angle and length measurements.

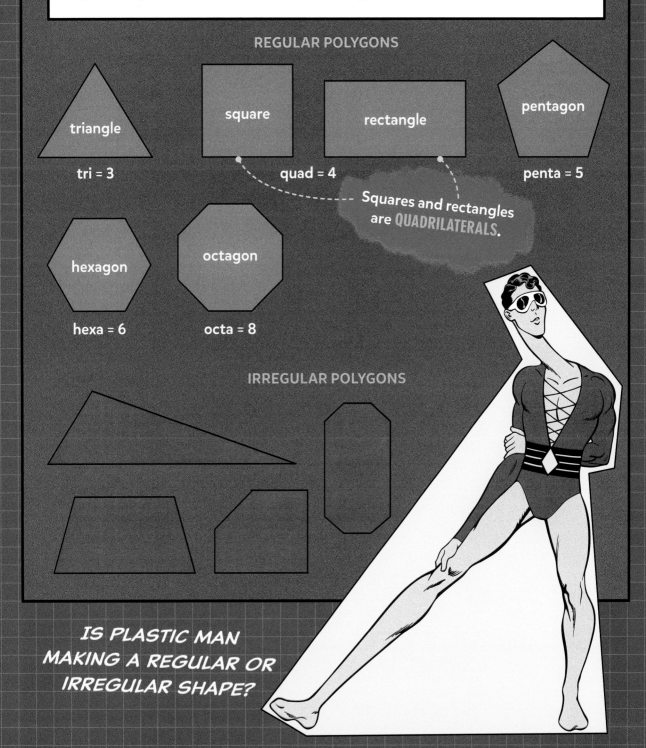

REGULAR POLYGONS

triangle

tri = 3

square

quad = 4

rectangle

Squares and rectangles are QUADRILATERALS.

pentagon

penta = 5

hexagon

hexa = 6

octagon

octa = 8

IRREGULAR POLYGONS

IS PLASTIC MAN MAKING A REGULAR OR IRREGULAR SHAPE?

PERIMETER

The **PERIMETER** is the length around the outside of a shape. In other words, it's the sum of the length of each side of a shape.

Each side of a square is the same length: **6 inches**.

To find the perimeter, add up the length of each side: **6 + 6 + 6 + 6 = 24 inches**

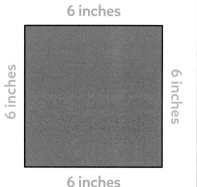

6 inches

6 inches

6 inches

6 inches

The length and width of a rectangle are two different amounts.

To find the perimeter of the rectangle, add up the length of each side:
3 + 7 + 3 + 7 = 20 inches

7 inches

3 inches

3 inches

7 inches

The Flash calculates the PERIMETER of the city to figure out how long it will take to get from one place to another.

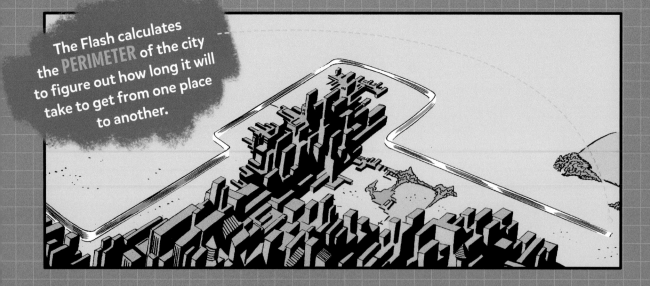

Try It!

Find the perimeter of each of these shapes.

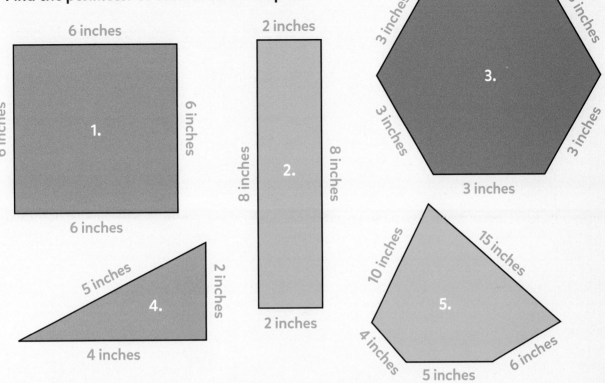

1. 6 inches (top), 6 inches (left), 6 inches (right), 6 inches (bottom)

2. 2 inches (top), 8 inches (left), 8 inches (right), 2 inches (bottom)

3. 3 inches (top), 3 inches, 3 inches, 3 inches, 3 inches, 3 inches

4. 5 inches, 2 inches, 4 inches

5. 10 inches, 15 inches, 4 inches, 5 inches, 6 inches

The Flash is fast, but sometimes he still wants to find the quickest route. If he had to run around the perimeter of each of these shapes, which would be the shortest?

Which would be the longest?

- -

Use the perimeter to figure out the missing length.

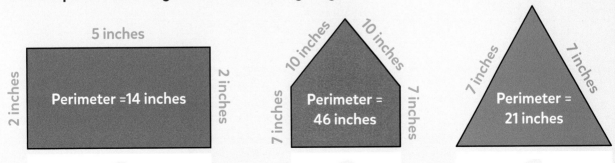

5 inches, 2 inches, 2 inches, Perimeter = 14 inches, ?

10 inches, 10 inches, 7 inches, 7 inches, Perimeter = 46 inches, ?

7 inches, 7 inches, Perimeter = 21 inches, ?

Answers on page 112.

AREA

Superman has the power to cool things down or heat things up. He might freeze a wall to make it easier to break or heat up a floor to make a villain hop! When he uses this power, he needs to know how much space, or **AREA**, to cover with his freeze breath or his heat vision.

Area is the amount of space a flat object takes up. One way Superman can figure out the area of the wall, floor, or other space is by counting.

Sometimes, Superman imagines a grid over the wall he wants to freeze. Each square on the grid represents one unit. In this case, each square represents **1** square foot. Square feet is one of the units used for area.

LENGTH

WIDTH

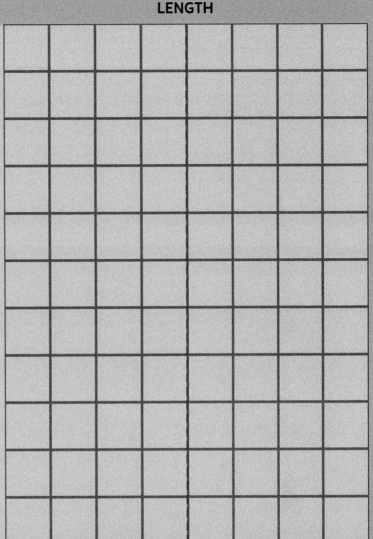

Superman can count each and every square in the grid. How many squares are there?

To make it easier to count, Superman can divide the wall into two equal parts by cutting it in half vertically. He then counts each square in one part, and doubles the number. If there are **44** squares in half the wall, then there are **44 × 2** or **88** squares—or square feet in the entire wall. Better get freezing!

For larger areas, counting by units might not be the fastest choice for Superman. If he wants to freeze an area the size of a football field, it would take a long time to count each unit square!

But Superman knows a trick so he doesn't have to count. He knows that the area of a rectangle can be found by multiplying the length of one of its short sides by the length of one of its long sides. The equation is **AREA = LENGTH × WIDTH**. In this case:

length = 150 yards

100 yards

width = 100 yards

150 yards

100 yards × 150 yards = 15,000 square yards

Area is measured in square units, like square centimeters, square inches, square feet, square yards, and square miles. Good thing Superman didn't need to count all those squares—he'd be counting for a while!

TO FIND AREA...

AREA = LENGTH × WIDTH

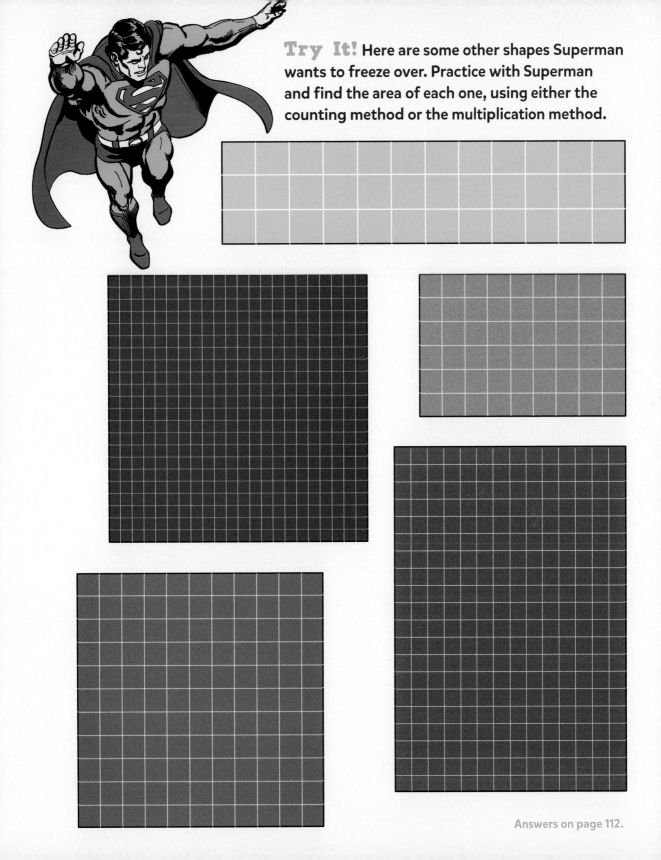

Try It! Here are some other shapes Superman wants to freeze over. Practice with Superman and find the area of each one, using either the counting method or the multiplication method.

Answers on page 112.

3D Shapes and Volume

With his power ring, Green Lantern can make anything out of light. Whether it is a giant hammer or a cage for captured villains, he makes three-dimensional shapes to save the day. If he can imagine it, Green Lantern can make it!

THREE-DIMENSIONAL (3D) shapes have **LENGTH**, **WIDTH**, and **HEIGHT**.

Most objects you interact with are **3D**. Some have special names, like cylinders or spheres. Others are different types of prisms.

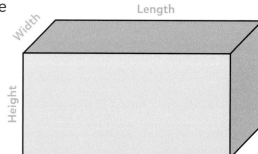

Instead of being a sphere like planet Earth, Bizarro World is a cube.

3D SHAPES

cube

rectangular prism or cuboid (a 3D rectangle)

cone

cylinder

sphere

triangular prism

triangular pyramid (tetrahedron)

pyramid

When Green Lantern makes a hammer, what type of shape is he making?

Three-dimensional shapes have **VOLUME**. Volume is the amount of space an object takes up. It can also refer to how much space is inside the object if it's hollow. For rectangular prisms, you can find the volume using a simple formula.

VOLUME OF A RECTANGULAR PRISM

LENGTH × WIDTH × HEIGHT = VOLUME

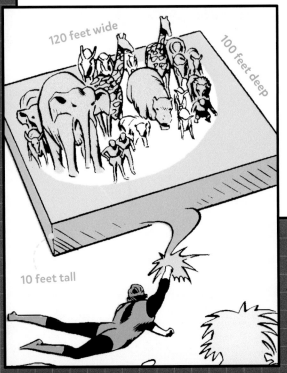

120 feet wide

100 feet deep

10 feet tall

Once, during an emergency, Green Lantern made a huge platform to carry animals to safety. To find the volume of the platform, multiply length by width by height:

120 × 100 × 10 = 120,000 CUBIC FEET

Cubic inches, cubic feet, cubic centimeters, and cubic meters are some measures of volume.

COORDINATE Planes

In the blink of an eye, Raven can vanish and reappear in a totally different place. Her teleportation powers let her surprise an enemy or carry others to safety. But to teleport, Raven has to know where she is and where she's going. She needs to know the distance between her starting point and her end point. It's a lot of information to keep track of!

One way Raven can know where she is and where she wants to go is by imagining a **COORDINATE PLANE.** A coordinate plane is made of a **y-AXIS**, which runs up and down, and an **x-AXIS**, which runs side to side.

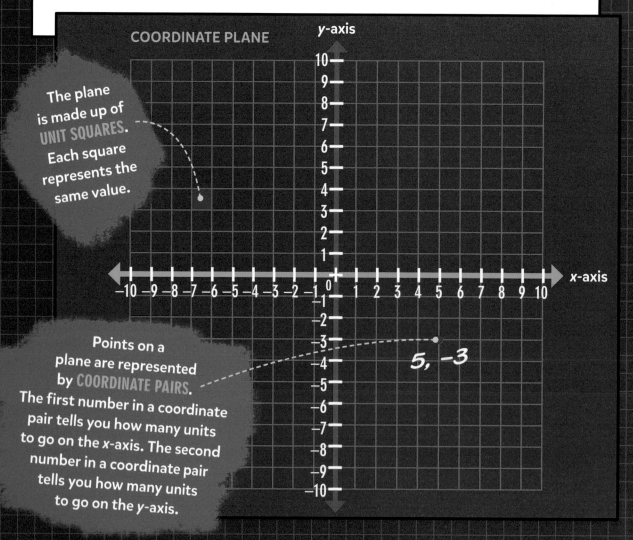

COORDINATE PLANE

The plane is made up of UNIT SQUARES. Each square represents the same value.

5, −3

Points on a plane are represented by COORDINATE PAIRS. The first number in a coordinate pair tells you how many units to go on the x-axis. The second number in a coordinate pair tells you how many units to go on the y-axis.

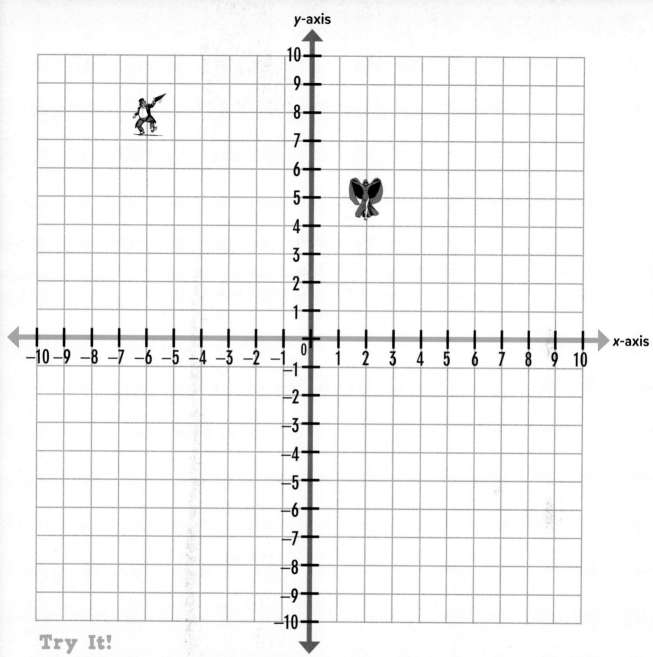

Try It!

1. Raven starts at 2, 5. She then teleports 2 units to the left and 1 unit down from where she started. What coordinate pair does she land on?

-----

2. From there, Raven wants to surprise Penguin on the coordinate plane. How many units will she need to travel horizontally (to the side)?

-----

3. Then, to bump right into Penguin, how many units would she need to travel vertically (up or down)?

Answers on page 112.

GRAPH IT!

When she isn't fighting crime as Batgirl, Barbara Gordon is a librarian. That means she's a great researcher. When Batgirl does research, she collects **DATA**. Data is another word for facts. By analyzing data, Batgirl can solve problems or understand situations.

There are many ways to collect data. There are also many ways to display it. To keep track of her data, Batgirl makes **TABLES** and **GRAPHS** to display it. A table is a bunch of facts arranged in rows and columns. There are three main types of graphs: line graphs, bar graphs, and circle graphs.

A **LINE GRAPH** shows a change in data over time. It might show how many criminals have been active month to month or how many Super Heroes are part of the Justice League from year to year.

Batgirl kept a record of how many crimes she prevented in Gotham City every month. She put her data in a **TABLE**.

CRIMES STOPPED BY BATGIRL IN GOTHAM CITY

MONTH	NUMBER OF CRIMES STOPPED
January	10
February	3
March	5
April	3
May	2
June	14
July	12
August	9
September	5
October	3
November	5
December	6

To put the data into a line graph, she labeled the *x*-axis, which is the horizontal axis, with the months. She labeled the *y*-axis, which runs vertically, or up and down, with the number of crimes stopped. Then she put a dot on the graph to represent each fact from the table. See how the dot for January represents the number 10?

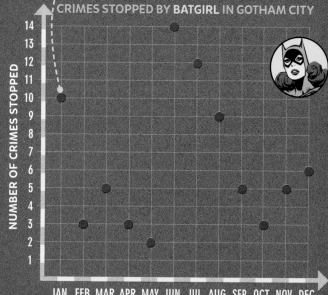

CRIMES STOPPED BY BATGIRL IN GOTHAM CITY

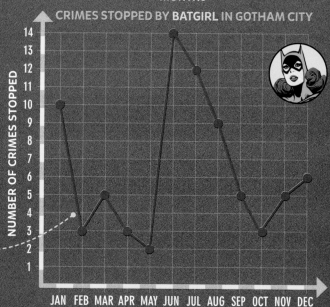

CRIMES STOPPED BY BATGIRL IN GOTHAM CITY

Then she connected the dots to create a line graph. Seeing her data in a line graph made it easy to see that she caught the most criminals in the summer.

Batgirl also collected data about how many crimes Batman and Robin stopped in Gotham City each month. She put that data in a table. Batgirl always remembers to put a title above her tables and graphs. You should too!

CRIMES STOPPED BY BATMAN AND ROBIN IN GOTHAM CITY

MONTH	NUMBER OF CRIMES STOPPED BY BATMAN	NUMBER OF CRIMES STOPPED BY ROBIN
January	6	7
February	11	4
March	9	5
April	12	7
May	14	1
June	6	9
July	4	8
August	7	11
September	8	2
October	3	3
November	10	6
December	8	2

She put her data about Batman and Robin into **LINE GRAPHS** too. First she put dots on the graphs to represent each fact from her chart. Then she drew lines to connect the dots. Line graphs make it easy to compare data.

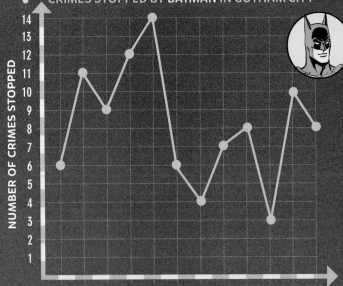

CRIMES STOPPED BY **BATMAN** IN GOTHAM CITY

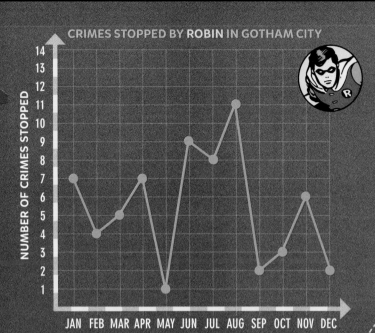

CRIMES STOPPED BY **ROBIN** IN GOTHAM CITY

NUMBER OF CRIMES STOPPED

14 13 12 11 10 9 8 7 6 5 4 3 2 1

JAN FEB MAR APR MAY JUN JUL AUG SEP OCT NOV DEC

MONTHS

You can also plot two line graphs on the same grid in different colors to compare data. Here, you can compare the number of crimes prevented by Batman and Robin each month.

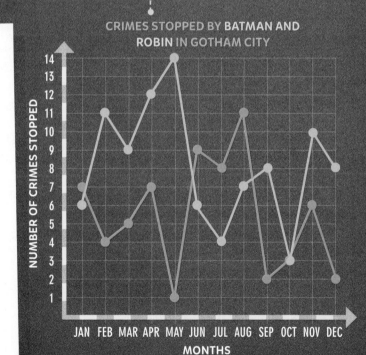

CRIMES STOPPED BY **BATMAN AND ROBIN** IN GOTHAM CITY

NUMBER OF CRIMES STOPPED

14 13 12 11 10 9 8 7 6 5 4 3 2 1

JAN FEB MAR APR MAY JUN JUL AUG SEP OCT NOV DEC

MONTHS

= BLUE LINE   = GREEN LINE

Try It! Batgirl can look at her graphs to answer questions about the data she collected. Can you answer her questions?

1. During which month did Batgirl stop the most crimes?

2. During which month did Batman stop the fewest crimes?

3. During which month did all three stop the same number of crimes?

Answers on page 112.

Not all of the data Batgirl collects makes sense as a line graph. Another thing she keeps track of is how many Super Heroes have different powers. It helps her know how many friends she can call on when she needs someone with a specific skill. After she collects her data, she organizes the data into a table.

SUPER HERO POWERS

POWER	NUMBER OF SUPER HEROES
Flight	61
Super-speed	92
Super-strength	150
Teleportation	20

Cyborg can use his teleportation powers to help people in a hurry.

In addition to super-speed, super-strength, heat vision, freeze breath, and X-ray vision, Supergirl has the power of flight!

The Flash uses his super-speed to race to the scene of any crime.

This data is best displayed as a **BAR GRAPH**. A bar graph compares the number of things there are in different categories. It could show how many Super Heroes wear a certain color suit or how many times different villains have tried to destroy the world.

To put the data into a BAR GRAPH, Batgirl labeled the *x*-axis with the superpowers. She labeled the *y*-axis with the number of Super Heroes. Then she drew a bar on the graph to represent each fact from the table. See how the bar for super-strength represents the number 150?

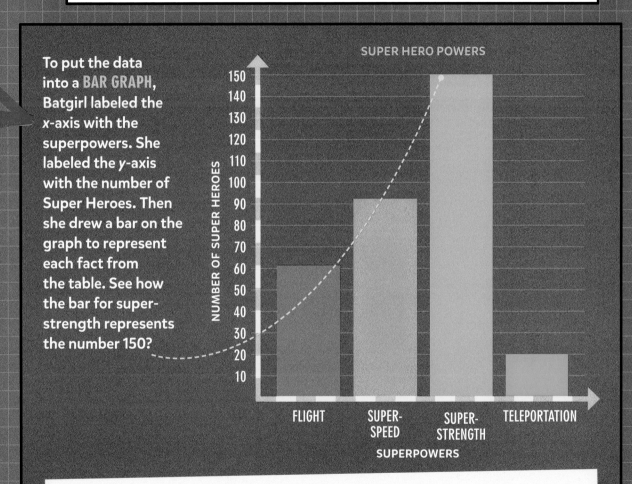

SUPER HERO POWERS

NUMBER OF SUPER HEROES

FLIGHT | SUPER-SPEED | SUPER-STRENGTH | TELEPORTATION

SUPERPOWERS

Try It! Batgirl uses her bar graph to answer the following questions:

1. What is the most common superpower?

2. What is the least common superpower?

3. How many Super Heroes can teleport?

What information would you put in a bar graph?

Answers on page 112.

Batgirl has even more graph tricks up her Super Hero suit's sleeve! One of her favorite questions to ask the citizens of different cities, like Gotham City and Metropolis, is who their favorite superhero is. She questioned **40** people in Gotham City and placed her data in a table.

Batgirl made this **CIRCLE GRAPH** after asking **40** people in Gotham City to name their favorite Super Hero.

GOTHAM CITY RESIDENTS' FAVORITE SUPER HEROES

SUPER HERO	NUMBER OF FANS
Batman	18
Batgirl	12
Robin	4
Nightwing	6

Then she chose the best type of graph to display the data. Each piece of data in this table can be read like this:

"18 out of 40 people said Batman was their favorite Super Hero."

or

"12 out of 40 people said Batgirl was their favorite Super Hero."

Each piece of data represents part of a whole. This kind of data can be displayed as a special type of graph called a **CIRCLE** or **PIE GRAPH**. They are also sometimes called pie charts.

A circle graph uses different wedges of a circle to represent the data. Since this graph shows the opinions given by **40** people, the circle is divided into **40** equal-sized wedges.

The circle graph shows at a glance which category is the biggest and which is the smallest. But remember—you can only use a circle graph when you're comparing parts of a whole!

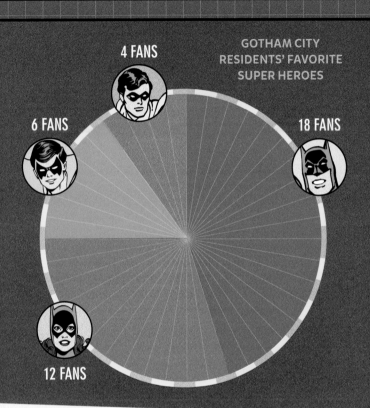

GOTHAM CITY RESIDENTS' FAVORITE SUPER HEROES

4 FANS

6 FANS

18 FANS

12 FANS

WHAT I DO IN 24 HOURS

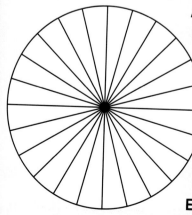

Try It! Collect your own data to make your own graph! Ask your friends which Super Hero they would most like to meet or which superpower they would most like to have.

You could also use a circle graph to show what you do in a day. Out of 24 hours, how many hours do you spend eating, sleeping, going to school, doing homework, participating in sports or other hobbies, reading books, and watching TV? First, put your data in a table. Then place it in a circle graph. To graph what you do all day, you can break up your circle into 24 equal wedges. Each wedge represents 1 hour. That way, it is easy to graph your data.

Tremendous TECHNOLOGY

Much of Cyborg's body is made of metal. He has an enhanced eye that lets him see things in greater detail than a normal human eye. He has sound cannons that can make powerful sonic blasts. And the computer parts in him can interact with other computers.

Cyborg is a feat of technology. Technology is knowledge or science put to use to solve problems. For example, a cell phone is a piece of technology used to solve the problem of staying in contact with others. And Cyborg's metal and computer parts were used to save his life after an accident. That was definitely a big problem!

WHAT TYPES OF TECHNOLOGY
CAN YOU THINK OF?

WHAT PROBLEMS DO THEY SOLVE?

THINK OF A PROBLEM IN THE WORLD THAT
NEEDS SOLVING. WHAT NEW TECHNOLOGY
COULD SOLVE IT?

ROBOTS at the Ready

Cyborg's technological parts help him do things he wouldn't be able to do otherwise. His metal arm is connected to the nerves in his shoulder. This lets him use his metal hand like a human hand. His computer eye can see like his human one. But it can also see in the dark and see heat signatures. These mechanical parts make Cyborg partially a robot.

IF THIS ROBOT WONDER WOMAN BEATS *ME*--SHE'LL WIN!

A robot is a machine that can do the work of a person or an animal. Robots can help producing things like cars. But they can also help in day-to-day life. Robots are everywhere!

HELPFUL ROBOTS

DRONES: Drones are a type of flying robot. Those with cameras can take photos or videos from overhead. Military drones are used to spy, to drop bombs, and to deliver supplies to hard-to-reach places. Drones are operated by a controller which sends radio signals from the drone's transmitter to its receiver.

RESCUE ROBOTS:

Some robots travel to places where humans can't or shouldn't go. Sophisticated rescue robots operate like Super Heroes! Some fight fires by blasting out tons of water from areas that are too hot and dangerous for humans. Others search for survivors of natural disasters like earthquakes or avalanches.

WORKER BOTS: You may have noticed robots in your local supermarket where they are busy cleaning floors, or making sure nobody steals. There are robots that pick crops faster than humans can. Robots can even perform surgery, controlled by a doctor sitting at a computer terminal, viewing the robot's magnified view of the surgical site.

ARTIFICIAL INTELLIGENCE
and Machine Learning

Cyborg's brain is as special as his body. It learns in a very unique way! Cyborg learns some things the same way any normal human would. But part of Cyborg's brain uses **ARTIFICIAL INTELLIGENCE** to control his machine parts. Artificial intelligence is what enables machines to decide what to do. When Cyborg's mechanical eye takes in information, it's learning what his surroundings are like. It then decides what information to relay to Cyborg, without having to be told what to do. And when the microphone in the computer side of his head picks up on a sound, his computer brain can automatically make the noise clearer and louder, translate it if it's in another language, or even identify it if it's an animal sound!

Cyborg's brain is special in another way. The computer side of it learns using **MACHINE LEARNING**. That means his computer brain works better the more he uses it. Every time he hears a sound, reads a book, or fights a battle, his computer brain gets smarter. It can better predict what Cyborg will need it to do.

Sometimes, when you're typing a message on a phone, it starts to fill in words as you type. That's an example of machine learning. Your text software pays attention to the words and phrases you type. The more it sees certain patterns, the more likely it is to suggest those words or phrases. TV and video streaming services also use machine learning. Often when you finish watching a show on a streaming platform, some recommendations for other shows will appear. The streaming platform's algorithm pays attention to the types of shows you like and finds shows with similar characteristics to suggest.

Think Like a COMPUTER

Brainiac's high-tech mental powers make him a dangerous Super-Villain.

Whenever you play a game on a tablet, text using a phone, or do homework on a computer, you're putting **COMPUTER CODE** to work. As a computer scientist, Batman knows a thing or two about computer code. He writes programs using different coding languages to tell computers what to do. Without code, his Batcave computer wouldn't work—and neither would yours!

A computer program is a collection of instructions that can be carried out by a computer to accomplish a task. They're written in programming languages that you can learn, just like you'd learn a foreign language. Lines of code make all the computers around us work.

CODING LANGUAGES

Coding languages are sets of commands that computer programmers use to tell a computer what to do. They're also called programming languages. There are many different coding languages. All of them can be used for most programs. But different coding languages are popular for different uses. C++ and Java are mostly used for making video games. HTML5 and CSS are used to make websites. And Python is a popular choice for just about anything!

In order to write code for a computer, you need to think like a computer. And computers think very literally! They can't fill in the gaps in an explanation like humans can. They do only what they're told to do in the exact order they're told to do it. They follow rules so closely that it can make them do silly things, or even make it so they can't finish their task at all!

Imagine writing code for a robot to pour a cup of orange juice. You would have to name every step, like this:

1) Open the cabinet door.
2) Pick up a cup.
3) Place the cup, right side up, on the counter.
4) Close the cabinet door.
5) Open the refrigerator door.
6) Pick up the orange juice container.
7) Close the refrigerator door.
8) Place the orange juice container on the counter.
9) Unscrew the top of the orange juice container.
10) Place the top of the orange juice container on the counter.
11) Pick up the orange juice container.
12) Pour the orange juice into the cup.
13) Put the orange juice container on the counter.
14) Screw the top back on the orange juice container.
15) Open the refrigerator door.
16) Pick up the orange juice container.
17) Place the orange juice container in the refrigerator.
18) Close the refrigerator door.
19) Pick up the cup of orange juice.
20) Drink the orange juice!

Try It! Imagine you're trying to explain to Martian Manhunter how to make a bowl of cereal. But, like a computer reading code, he'll only do exactly what you tell him to do. He's never had cereal before! Write out a numbered list of instructions. Be specific. Remember, if you skip anything, Martian Manhunter won't do it!

After you've written your instructions, test them out. Were you able to make a bowl of cereal by following only your instructions? If not, fill in your missing steps and try again.

ALOGORITHMS

As the leader of a team, Green Lantern has to give very clear instructions. If his instructions aren't clear enough, his team will be confused and possibly make a mistake. If he uses the wrong terms, his team could do the wrong thing. But if he tells his team what to do in easy-to-understand steps, using the right terms, then his team will perform perfectly!

IT'S MY OLD FOE, SINESTRO--

The same is true for computers. When telling a computer what to do, computer programmers need to give good instructions. That's why they write **ALGORITHMS**. Algorithms are instructions telling a computer what to do. Each task a computer does is controlled by one algorithm. It can take many, many algorithms working together to make a program!

Do you have a bedtime routine? You can think of it like an algorithm! First, put on your pajamas. Then you brush your teeth. You set your alarm, then climb to bed. You read two comic books, then lie down, close your eyes, and go to sleep. Each step in your routine is an instruction that leads up to the moment when you close your eyes. All those instructions together make an algorithm!

Algorithms are made up of coding building blocks. Here are some of the most common ones used.

- **VARIABLES** are placeholders that represent a value.

- **LOOPS** are pieces of code that repeat over and over again, until a certain condition is met. A loop might instruct a computer to print "I'M BATMAN" over and over, up to 10 times.

- **CONDITIONALS** are if/then statements. They're pieces of code that say, "If a given condition is true, then the computer will do a certain thing." It might be "If a password is correctly input, then files will be accessible."

- **FUNCTIONS** are blocks of code that are written to do one specific thing. They're reusable, so if a coder writes a function once, they can reuse it again and again. For example, when the function *DOUBLE(input)* is used, it will call up a block of code that multiplies whatever the input is by 2. The input is a variable that can be changed to whatever number the programmer wants.

BINARY CODE
The earliest computer programs were punch cards written in binary code. Today, when people write code, they write it using programming languages. But before a computer can follow code written by people, it translates the code into binary first. Binary code is made up of 0s and 1s. It's the only language computers really understand! Different combinations of 0s and 1s give precise instructions to the computer.

IF I BECOME
a Super Hero, Then I Will . . .

Two-Face is a Super-Villain who lets a coin flip make his decisions. If the coin lands on heads, then he'll do one thing. If the coin lands on tails, then he'll do a different thing. Two-Face's actions are conditional. They are determined by the outcome of the coin flip.

Computers often work just like Two-Face (except for being evil). Computer programs often include **CONDITIONAL STATEMENTS**. These if/then statements tell the computer to do one thing if a given value is true and to do a different thing if a given value is false. They have the computer check if a given condition is met. If the condition is met, then the computer performs an action.

When fighting crime and stopping Super-Villains, Super Heroes use conditional statements too! It's almost like they are "programmed" to take certain actions **IF** they encounter certain situations.

IF THERE IS A RUNAWAY TRAIN, THEN WONDER WOMAN MUST STOP IT.

IF A PLANE IS IN DANGER, THEN CLARK KENT MUST BECOME SUPERMAN.

IF BATMAN SEES THE BAT-SIGNAL, THEN HE MUST GO HELP GOTHAM CITY.

Try It! Write a conditional statement telling the Super Heroes what they need to do if certain conditions are met.

LOGIC

LOGIC is a reasonable, orderly way of thinking about something. And Earth logic is still new to Starfire.

To understand information, she might use a **VENN DIAGRAM**. A Venn diagram is a way to organize and compare information using two or more overlapping circles.

One way Starfire can use a Venn diagram is to compare and contrast the characteristics of two people. For example, how are she and Beast Boy different? How are they the same? She labels each circle and then writes their differences in each circle. Where the circles overlap, she writes their similarities.

STARFIRE   BEAST BOY

Each circle is the "or" part of an and/or statement.

- Has energy blasts
- Is orange
- Is an alien

- Part of the Teen Titans
- Can fly

- Can shape-shift
- Is green
- Is a human

The overlapping parts of a Venn diagram are the "and" parts of an and/or statement.

Computers also understand this type of and/or logic. And/or commands are used in creating computer code. The words "and" and "or" are also very helpful for anyone using a computer to search for information. Including "and" will only turn up information about both items searched. Using "or" will turn up information on both independently. It's one more example of computers being super logical!

Try It! Train your brain to organize information just like a computer does.

Help Starfire learn more about plants by helping her figure out which of these items are foods and/or plants. Put these words where they belong on the Venn diagram:
tomatoes, pretzels, daisies, roses, cheese, lettuce, cucumbers, carrots, corn, oak tree, yogurt, grass, tacos, sunflowers

FOODS   **PLANTS**

Which of these characters wears a cape and/or wears red boots? Put them where they belong in the Venn diagram.

WEARS A CAPE   **WEARS RED BOOTS**
BOTH

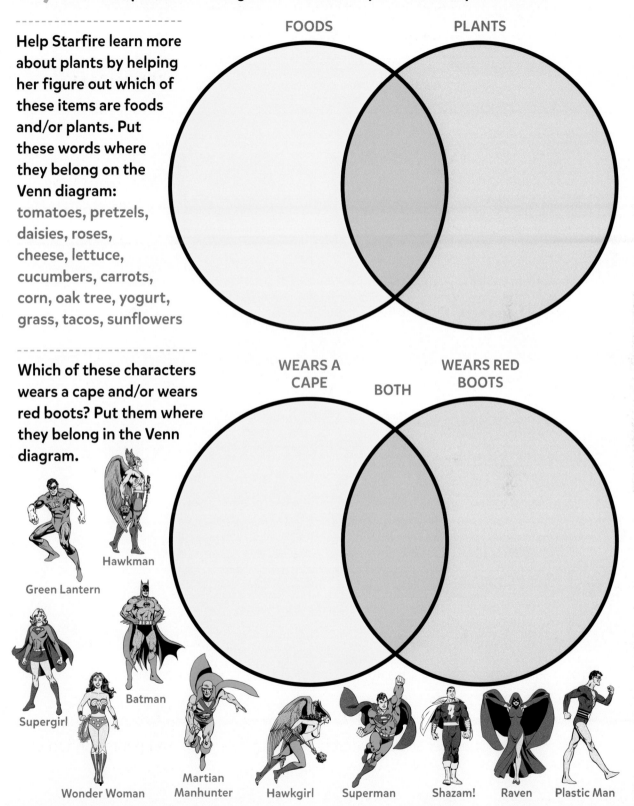

Green Lantern

Hawkman

Supergirl

Wonder Woman

Batman

Martian Manhunter

Hawkgirl

Superman

Shazam!

Raven

Plastic Man

The Wonders of WI-FI

When Batman needs to do some quick research, he uses the internet—just like you do! All he has to do is search a few keywords, and the information he needs turns up.

WI-FI is a wireless way to access the internet. It lets you access information stored around the world by turning that information into radio signals.

When Batman types a question into his browser, it turns into a radio wave. His router sends that radio wave out to servers that store information. Those servers then locate the information he wants and send back a radio wave that his router can understand. That radio wave is then translated into a web page full of text and pictures. Hopefully the web page answers Batman's questions.

Wi-Fi signals cover a wide area. If Batman wants to wander from room to room in his mansion, he can still access the internet using Wi-Fi from his laptop. But some gadgets, like wireless video game controllers or wireless headsets, trade signals more directly. This is point-to-point communication: from the game controller to a game console, or from a music player to the headset. The radio waves are being exchanged in the same way as Wi-Fi though.

Wireless communication using Wi-Fi is a powerful way to stay in touch. But it is not always the most secure. Batgirl is an expert hacker— that means she can use special computer skills to get to data that's protected. She only uses her skills for good, but other hackers try to steal information that can hurt her or her friends. That's why she makes sure her team is careful when using the internet!

WEB SAFETY

The internet can be a powerful tool, but remember to stay safe! Be like a Super Hero and never give out your real name or your passwords. Don't share your age or where you live either. When you're on the internet, keep your secret identity a secret!

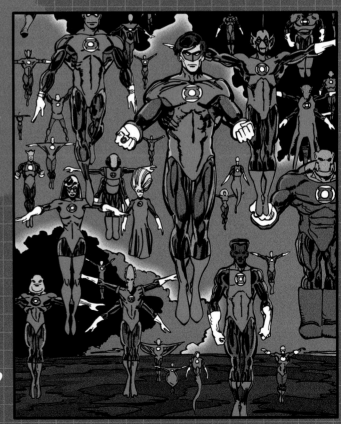

SOME SUPER HEROES, LIKE THE GREEN LANTERNS, DON'T NEED THE INTERNET TO COMMUNICATE. THEY USE TELEPATHY!

ALL Connected

On the Justice League's space station, there's lots of technology. Computers trace the station's path, monitors track who enters or leaves, and the kitchen's fridge even knows what food is available and what's running low—the most important data, according to The Flash!

The space station is an example of the **INTERNET OF THINGS**. Each piece of technology in the station can communicate with the other parts of the station using the internet. The station also shares information with Martian Manhunter, Superman, Wonder Woman, and other members of the Justice League so they always know what's happening up in space. Even when the heroes are on Earth, they can control the movements and settings of the space station. No need to worry if they left the TV on when they rushed out the door!

But the team has to be careful to keep their station secure. Because the Internet of Things relies on internet communication to work, it can be a way for sneaky people to access their information. A Super-Villain might hack into their smart fridge to listen in on the League's plans or put spyware, a dangerous type of computer software, onto their computer to capture their passwords. Lucky for the Justice League, several Super Heroes are computer whizzes.

Computer experts, like Martian Manhunter and Batgirl, use many tactics to keep their computers—and the information on them—safe! They use firewalls to keep villains out. Firewalls let only certain people at certain times access their information. They set up their computers and machines so that every user has a password. Sometimes their electronics even require a fingerprint, a retina scan (your retina is part of your eye), or facial recognition to log on. This type of protection is called **CYBERSECURITY**.

Other technology designed to keep your information safe includes keystroke analysis. A keystroke program can track a person's behavior. It may note how fast a user usually types or where a device is usually used in order to detect if someone else is using a person's device.

Everyday TECH

When you think of technology, you might think of the Justice League's computers on their space station or Batman's crime-fighting gadgets. But tech isn't just computers or machines! From brushing your teeth to tying your shoes, you're using technology.

THE SIGNAL WAS SWEEPING TOWARD THE NEW AIR TERMINAL! SOMEONE THERE MUST HAVE PHONED IN AN ALARM!

WE CAN BE THERE IN MINUTES!

In fact, before Batman uses any of his gadgets, he uses a different type of tech. He drives out of the Batcave using a **TUNNEL**!

Tunnels are tubes hollowed out of dirt or stone. The machines that make them are also feats of technology! Construction workers use spinning drills to move mounds of rock and dirt. Once built, tunnels have to withstand a lot of pressure. Dirt, rock, or water press on them from all sides. They're one of the biggest challenges for engineers.

The reason tunnels are so strong is because they're one long ARCH. Arches have a curved shape that evenly distributes pressure. That means there's no weak spots or places under more pressure that might break and cause the tunnel to collapse.

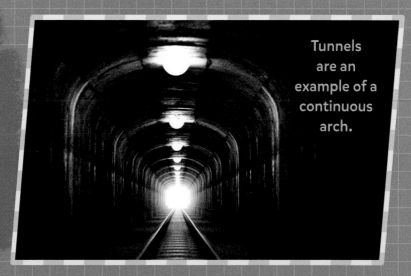

Tunnels are an example of a continuous arch.

BRIDGES also use technology. Bridges stay up by relying on compression and tension. Compression is when something is squeezed together or made smaller. Tension is a force that pulls something in a direction. Here are four common types of bridges used today.

A **BEAM BRIDGE** is the most basic bridge. It is made up of planks of wood or stone called beams. These beams are balanced on supports called piers or abutments. The beams compress the piers to stay up.

A **TRUSS BRIDGE** is similar to a beam bridge but adds a truss. A truss helps support the beams. It's a structure often made of triangles that wall the bridge in. The truss provides both compression and tension. It distributes stress more evenly.

ARCH BRIDGES are built in the shape of an arch. That means the bridge is constantly compressing itself, which holds it up. Stress is evenly distributed along the arch.

SUPERMAN DOESN'T NEED A BRIDGE TO CROSS A RIVER— HE CAN JUST FLY!

Tall piers form towers that support a **SUSPENSION BRIDGE**. Cables run from these piers that connect to the bridge below and brace it. The bridge presses down on the piers and is held up by tension from the cables.

HIGH-RISE How-To

Superman can jump over tall buildings —even skyscrapers! These towering buildings reach hundreds of feet into the air.

Architects and engineers use a combination of age-old technology and cutting-edge ideas to design buildings that reach high in the sky. High-rises are tall and heavy, so they need a very supportive foundation. A foundation is what a structure is built on. A high-rise's foundation is made of heavy concrete. It's anchored into the ground to give it even more sturdiness. The frame of a high-rise is usually made of steel and concrete, carefully built up using cranes and scaffolds.

Many skyscrapers are a little bit like the great pyramids built thousands of years ago. They are wider at the base and get thinner as they go up. The large base supports the smaller sections higher up.

Because they're so tall, high-rises also need to be able to sway! A high-rise's steel and concrete skeleton has just enough give to move with wind and any tremors in the earth.

Taiwan is hit by typhoons—even Superman might struggle to fly through these windy storms! So TAIPEI 101, an incredibly tall building in Taiwan, was specially constructed to stand up to strong winds. The building's architects gave it a large swinging weight called a mass damper. When the building sways one way, the mass damper sways in the other direction. This hefty weight keeps the tall tower from toppling!

The tallest skyscraper in the world is the BURJ KHALIFA in the United Arab Emirates. It's 2,717 feet tall! Unlike Taipei 101, it doesn't have a mass damper. Instead, its design borrows an idea from nature. Instead of being one tall cylinder or prism, the building is shaped like a three-petaled flower. Wind easily swirls around the building's curved, Y-shaped sides.

Floor plan

Elevators are technology too! They solve the problem of getting people and things up and down. The GUANGZHOU CTF FINANCE TOWER in China has an elevator that travels at 46 miles per hour!

Signals from SPACE

What's that way, way up in the air? It's Superman. He's in space flying around the Earth. But there's something else. A satellite! **SATELLITES** are objects that revolve around a larger object in space. The moon is a natural satellite of Earth. Artificial satellites are made by humans to do many different jobs. They can send information around the world in seconds. You might not even realize it, but you use satellites every day.

Satellites work by bouncing signals around the world. A ground station on Earth sends a signal into space. The satellite receives the signal and bounces it to a receiver on the Earth. This all happens very quickly and across huge distances—sometimes from one side of the Earth to the other in a matter of seconds!

SATELLITE

GROUND STATION

RECEIVER

Scientists use satellites to take pictures of planets, asteroids, and even black holes deep in space. Sometimes they use photos taken from satellites in space to learn about things on Earth. They can locate archaeological sites or measure mountains or glaciers from space!

Satellites can also capture the movements of storm clouds. When Superman checks the weather report before taking off, he's relying on predictions made based on pictures and information collected by satellites.

When Superman calls up Hawkgirl to check in on a mission in a remote place, he can use a satellite phone. They work in places where there aren't cell phone towers. Because satellites send signals so fast, Superman and Hawkgirl can have a conversation like they're standing side by side—even if they're on opposite sides of the world.

When Super Heroes relax by watching fun TV shows, their TV sets are picking up signals sent from a satellite!

Wonder Woman can use satellite technology to communicate with others while she zooms around the world in her Invisible Jet.

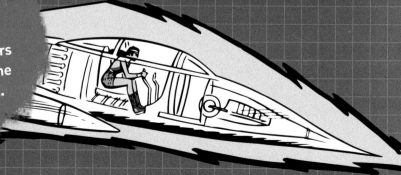

GPS Shows You the Way

FINALLY...

MADE IT--AT LAST! I HOPE THAT DELAY WASN'T **COSTLY!**

As he zooms around the globe, The Flash can get a little lost. He moves so fast he isn't always sure where he is! Lucky for him, he can check his location on his phone. His phone is a **GPS** receiver. GPS stands for **GLOBAL POSITIONING SYSTEM**.

The GPS is a network of more than **30** satellites in space. As long as The Flash and his GPS receiver are within range of four of the GPS satellites, he can find out where he is. Radio waves from the GPS satellites travel through both space and the air to his receiver. The receiver can calculate how long it took the radio waves to reach it from each of the nearest GPS satellites. Using that information, it can figure out how far away those satellites are. The satellites' locations are well known. So if The Flash's GPS receiver knows that it is a certain distance from each of four satellites, it can do a complicated math problem to find its own location on Earth. It does all of those calculations in a matter of seconds. And The Flash thinks *he's* speedy!

GPS is most often used for pinpointing locations. It helps people navigate from one location to another, track the movement of people and packages, and make and improve maps. GPS is used in other neat ways too!

Some PET COLLARS contain a tracker that's connected to GPS. If your pet gets lost, GPS can track them and help you reunite with your furry friend!

GAMES on your phone can use GPS to match up where you are with what you see in the game.

GPS can even save your life. EMERGENCY SERVICES can track your phone to find you if you need medical help or if you get lost while hiking or skiing.

...NOTHING!

LIVING in SPACE

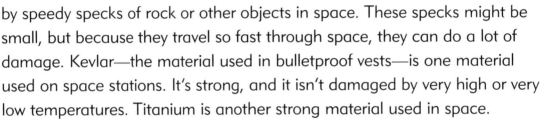

The Justice League's **SPACE STATION** gives the team a home base in space. From it, members of the Justice League can keep an eye on Earth.

The space station itself has to keep the team safe. That means its walls need to stop dangerous radiation from space. It also needs to be strong enough to withstand being hit by speedy specks of rock or other objects in space. These specks might be small, but because they travel so fast through space, they can do a lot of damage. Kevlar—the material used in bulletproof vests—is one material used on space stations. It's strong, and it isn't damaged by very high or very low temperatures. Titanium is another strong material used in space.

These materials are lightweight too. Why does a space station need to be lightweight? To make it easier to get its pieces into space! It takes a lot of power to lift heavy things into space. That's why the outside of many parts of a space station is made of lightweight aluminum. Layers of ceramic tile are used too. They protect spacecraft from the sun's intense heat.

The International Space Station (ISS) orbits Earth.

The ISS is a space station like the Justice League's. When the Justice League's station needs repairs, Martian Manhunter can fly into space to fix it. But when human astronauts need to make repairs, they wear carefully designed space suits and use robotic arms.

Astronauts keep months of food on the ISS. But uncrewed capsules can bring deliveries to the station. These capsules are launched on reusable rockets that gently land instead of crashing into the ocean.

SPACE INNOVATION ON EARTH

The ISS might seem like out-of-this-world tech. But people on Earth use a lot of same things that the astronauts use! Here are some things we wouldn't have without space exploration:

CAMERA PHONE technology was first developed so lightweight cameras on spacecraft could take high-resolution photos.

Engineers set out to create a rock-hard protective coating for a space station. They failed. But they succeeded in inventing a coating that keeps **EYEGLASSES** scratch-free.

Wires get tangled easily in space, so NASA designed **WIRELESS HEADSETS** so astronauts could communicate without having to deal with wires.

Magic of MATERIALS

There are many types of materials used to build houses, machines, and more. Your house might be made out of wood and brick, for example. Wood is lightweight and useful for building frames. Brick is heavy and sturdy, and can last for a long time.

BRICK WALLS ARE STRONG, BUT THEY'RE NO MATCH FOR THE FLASH!

Aquaman's kingdom of Atlantis is deep under the ocean. Every castle, tower, and building in Atlantis needs to be able to last in water. That means they need to be built out of water-resistant materials, like steel, concrete, and acrylic, which is a type of plastic.

NOW IT IS SAFE! HAD THE DEPTH BOMBS GONE OFF, THE ANCESTRAL HOME OF MY MOTHER... THE LAND OF ATLANTIS... WOULD HAVE BEEN DESTROYED FOREVER! PERHAPS, SOME DAY... I WILL RETURN HERE! WHO KNOWS?

New high-tech materials are being developed all the time. They are used to build stronger, safer, more environmentally friendly building materials. New materials are also used to make things like computers and smartphones run faster than ever!

PROBLEM-SOLVING MATERIALS

GRAPHENE: This ultra-strong material is made up of a single layer of atoms. It's stronger than steel! It's incredibly thin and conducts electricity and heat.

TRANSPARENT ALUMINUM: This super-strong substance may be better than a force field! An alloy or mixture of aluminum, oxygen, and nitrogen, it is transparent like glass, but nearly as hard as a sapphire. It can be used in extra-sturdy windows—and someday soon in vehicles for space or undersea exploration.

MUSHROOM MATERIAL: Protecting delicate things in the mail can be wasteful. But not if it's packaged in mushroom material! Several eco-conscious companies have created ways to make packaging and more out of mushrooms. It fully biodegrades, which means it breaks down in nature. Mushroom-based material is being used to make furniture and clothing too!

Every Super Hero has a stylish suit to keep them safe while fighting. But how can a piece of clothing stand up to the speeds at which Hawkgirl flies or protect her from attacks?

Fabric can be a type of technology too! If Hawkgirl needs a flexible suit, she'll pick a stretchy but strong type of fabric, like spandex, which can stretch to four times its original size!

If she wants her suit to tell her information about her environment, like the temperature, she'll pick a smart fabric. **SMART FABRICS** can help her with wind resistance by being incredibly smooth. They can also have teeny-tiny sensors embedded in them that track her heart rate, her body temperature, and more.

But what if she needs to suit up for extreme conditions? Some fabrics are lined with lead, which is a heavy metal, so they can stop radiation from penetrating the suit. Layered fabric is used in space suits to keep astronauts safe from the heat and radiation of space. When Hawkgirl suits up, it's not just for style!

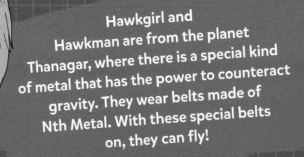

Hawkgirl and Hawkman are from the planet Thanagar, where there is a special kind of metal that has the power to counteract gravity. They wear belts made of Nth Metal. With these special belts on, they can fly!

The technology in The Flash's suit is incredible. The material is aerodynamic (that means it is designed to move swiftly through the air). It protects The Flash from extreme heat and cold. And the suit can shrink down to be tiny enough to fit in a ring he wears on his finger!

Lex Luthor needed a lot of money and Kryptonian technology to create a war suit with superpowers.

PROBLEM-SOLVING MATERIALS

SMARTY PANTS: Scientists and designers are developing technology such as vibrating fitness clothing that shows your muscles which way to move, yoga pants that help you optimize your poses, and a swimsuit that lets you know when you've had too much UV sun exposure.

GREEN FOOTWEAR: Like Poison Ivy, who works to protect plant life, many eco-conscious researchers are working to develop green technology. Many shoe companies now manufacture shoes made entirely from recycled ocean plastic, plastic bottles, fishing nets, and rubber.

Tough and TINY

Atom knows that tiny things can be very powerful. Atom can even shrink down to see microscopic molecules at work. **NANOTECHNOLOGY** involves manipulating material at a molecular level or nanoscale. Things that are **100** times smaller than the width of a single strand of hair (or even smaller) are measured in nanometers.

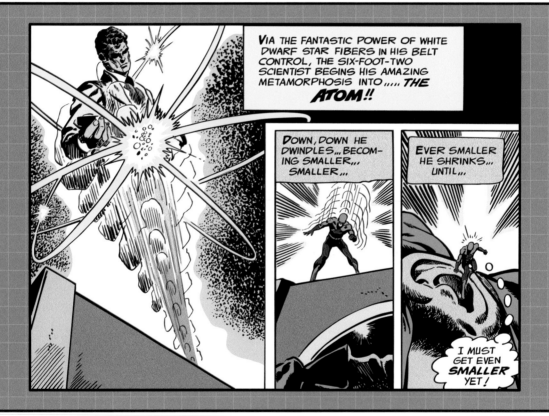

Engineers and inventors can make powerful technology by developing new materials at the atomic level. Clothing with carbon nano tubes woven into its fibers can be super-strong. Extremely thin films over glasses, lenses, and windows can keep glass extra-clean. A different type of coating can make lenses light- or heat-sensitive. So windows or sunglasses could automatically change from clear to dark to block out sunlight.

Medicine can also be made using nanotechnology. Traditional medicines travel through the blood stream. They don't target a specific part of the body, so sometimes they take a long time to work. And sometimes, a patient may take a dose that is higher or lower than what they actually need. Medications made using nanotechnology can target only the injured or sick cells in a body. That means there are fewer side effects. Scientists are experimenting with using nanoparticles to treat cancer. This type of nanomedicine would attach directly to tumors inside the body.

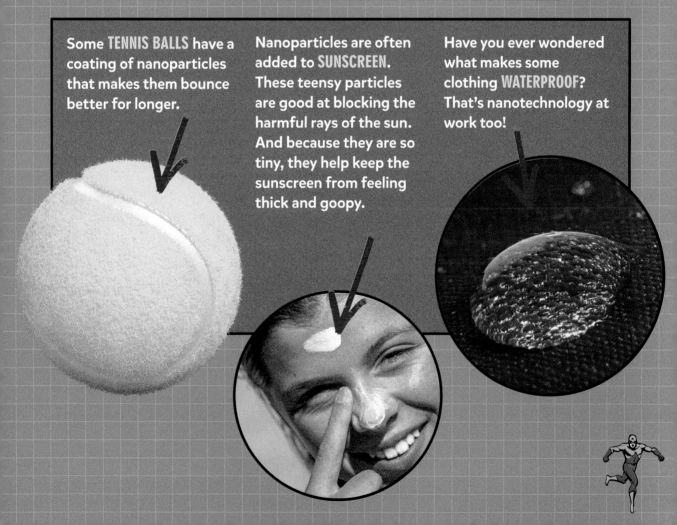

Some **TENNIS BALLS** have a coating of nanoparticles that makes them bounce better for longer.

Nanoparticles are often added to **SUNSCREEN**. These teensy particles are good at blocking the harmful rays of the sun. And because they are so tiny, they help keep the sunscreen from feeling thick and goopy.

Have you ever wondered what makes some clothing **WATERPROOF**? That's nanotechnology at work too!

PROTOTYPES and 3D PRINTING

Batman and Robin use lots of tools to fight crime. They're always on top of cutting-edge crime-fighting technology! Along with Lucius and Alfred, they make all their own Batarangs. They're constantly tweaking their designs and the materials they use to make better, more effective Batarangs.

A **PROTOTYPE** is an early form of an invention. It's made to show that a concept can work. Once a prototype is made and tested, it becomes the basis for future versions. By working with a prototype, Batman can decide if a different type of material would be better, and Robin can tell if a new Batarang flies far enough. Lucky for the team, they can use **3D PRINTERS** to make their prototypes.

A 3D printer makes a plastic prototype.

First, an inventor uses a computer to design a model. Then they print out the object. 3D printers often create objects out of plastic, but they can use many different materials. They can even print metal objects!

Some printers use beams of single electrons. These tiny, precise beams can make extremely detailed objects. Other printers use lasers to carefully remove material from a block to create an object instead of adding bits of material to build an object. A 3D-printed design can be adjusted easily and printed multiple times. Inventors, like Batman and Robin, can keep tweaking their designs until they get exactly what they want.

3D printers can make anything from toys to shoes!

With a 3D printer at the ready, Super-Villain Captain Boomerang is able to produce many boomerangs.

I HAD TO TURN CAPTAIN BOOMERANG LOOSE TO HELP THE ELONGATED MAN AND ME DEAL WITH THIS ALIEN INVASION OF EARTH! BUT ONCE IT'S OVER, HE'S GOING TO JAIL!

Tech of the FUTURE

Wizard's flying chair relies on magic, but in the future, floating chairs might use powerful magnets to defy gravity!

Scientists are constantly making new discoveries. That means technology is getting better and more innovative every day! Computers are becoming faster as researchers find new ways to make small, powerful electronics. Companies are perfecting self-driving cars. Clean energy, made from wind or water power, is replacing forms of energy that pollute the planet. And traveling to outer space is becoming more common.

Things you think of as science fiction—or the stuff of Super Heroes—might someday be reality too. High-tech cybernetic parts like Cyborg's could soon let people control their computers or phones with just their thoughts. The clothing The Flash wears that can stand up to intense heat and pressure could one day be worn by athletes or astronauts. And the artificial gravity found in the Justice League's space station might help permanent colonies stay grounded on Mars.

Just ask Booster Gold—a Super Hero from the future! His futuristic gadgets allow him to fly and travel through time. What do you think the technology of tomorrow will let you do?

Scientists are already working on fabric that reflects light to hide the person wearing it—just like this cloak of invisibility!

Window seats on planes are popular. That's why some aerospace engineers are trying to come up with ways to have a lot more windows on a plane. Who knows? Maybe sometime soon you'll be able to sightsee from the sky like these high-tech villains.

Jet packs exist. They are like rocket-powered backpacks that enable a person to fly. There are also special devices that use water-jets to let people hover in the air over water. But skis that enable people to fly? Those haven't been invented . . . yet. Stay tuned!

Scientists have cloned animals, like sheep, cows, rabbits, dogs, and horses. A Batman clone could stop twice as many villains!

ANSWERS

p. 15 1. –3, 2. 7, 3. 3

p. 17 1. 9, 2. 8, 3. 8

p. 20 1. 3, 2. 3

p. 23

1. 14 arrows – 10 targets = ___

2. 3 groups × 5 arrows = ___

3. 6 Super Heroes ÷ 3 groups = ___

p. 24–25

1. 68 inches – 62 inches = 6 inches

2. 5 costume parts × 7 days of the week = 35 costume parts

3. 8 Super Heroes ÷ 4 prisons = 2 Super Heroes in each prison

4. 4,000 pounds ÷ 100 people = 40 pounds per person

p. 27

The Flash's even-number path

2	7	15	12	4	9	40	6	22	12	89	7	90	14	74
44	2	78	12	5	14	30	37	12	7	8	10	68	39	96
9	45	17	4	65	12	11	27	88	50	12	31	12	41	100
12	13	81	8	77	66	21	98	13	71	55	24	8	91	11
5	7	11	12	20	54	33	2	6	12	79	99	47	75	85

Aquaman's odd-number path

12	7	15	12	4	10	87	6	22	12	13	93	45	9	50
44	2	78	64	5	77	79	37	12	7	17	16	68	39	6
1	45	17	4	65	12	2	27	88	55	12	31	12	41	22
12	10	81	90	77	66	21	35	13	71	40	24	8	91	9
5	7	11	13	21	54	83	2	6	64	79	33	20	56	99

p. 41

1. $\frac{3}{6} \div \frac{3}{3} = \frac{1}{2}$ inch

2. $\frac{10}{2} \div \frac{2}{2} = \frac{5}{1} = 5$ inches

3. $\frac{15}{30} \div \frac{15}{15} = \frac{1}{2}$ inch

4. $\frac{4}{16} \div \frac{4}{4} = \frac{1}{4}$ inch

p. 47

Superman: 6'3", Krypto: 2'4", Batman: 6'2", Hawkgirl: 5'4", Wonder Woman: 6', Green Lantern: 6'2", Martian Manhunter: 6'7", Batgirl: 5'11", Penguin: 5'2"

p. 49

Farenheit: 150°F, Celsius: 65°C

p. 53

acute angles = ○   obtuse angles = ○
right angles = ○

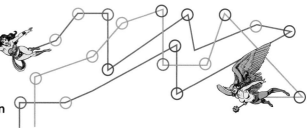

p. 57

1. 24", 2. 20", 3. 18", 4. 11", 5. 40"

shortest = 4. (triangle)

longest = 5. (irregular pentagon)

Missing side: rectangle = 5", pentagon = 12", triangle = 7"

p. 61

green: 3 × 12 = 36 units

blue: 22 × 22 = 484 units

orange: 6 × 9 = 54 units

purple: 11 × 11 = 121 units

red: 14 × 20 = 280 units

p. 65

1. $x = 0$, $y = 4$

2. 6 units (to go from 0 to –6)

3. 4 units (to go from 4 to 8)

p. 69

1. June 2. October 3. October

p. 71

1. super-strength 2. teleportation 3. 20